"Sometimes I think Michael doesn't understand a word I say." Does that have a familiar ring? If you seem to be having trouble getting your messages across to your child, maybe it's not his or her fault. Remember, children are not born with the ability to *listen*, only with the ability to *hear*. Remember also, that parents often don't know how to listen either! If your child persists in unacceptable behavior, the roots are nearly always to be found in poor listening habits. You may unwittingly be contributing to this yourself, by giving abtract or confusing messages to your child—"Don't dilly-dally," "Be good!"—You may be using vague or misleading words to your child and providing confusing cues.

Child psychologist Tom Banville has written this book to help both you and your child develop your communication skills, and so reach a better understanding.

Also by Thomas J. Banville, Ph. D.:

How to Listen—How to be Heard

HOW TO GET YOUR CHILD TO LISTEN

THOMAS J. BANVILLE, PH.D.

CONDOR

NEW YORK

HOW TO GET YOUR CHILD TO LISTEN

CONDOR

PRINTING HISTORY
CONDOR edition published June 1978

ISBN 0-89516-034-X
Library of Congress Catalog Number: 78-53465

Printed by the United States of America

CONDOR PUBLISHING COMPANY, INC.
521 Fifth Avenue
New York, N.Y. 10017

For Jack Rose, who understood the Muse better than I. But for him this book might never have been written.

Contents

HOW TO GET
YOUR CHILD
TO LISTEN

PREFACE

WHEN I talk with parents about behavior problems, I almost always hear the complaint that "Johnny doesn't listen." When I talk with Johnny, he has the same complaint about mother and dad: "I try to talk with them, but they just don't listen."

Experience tells me that Johnny doesn't listen because he doesn't know *how* to listen. He doesn't know how because his parents didn't teach him how.

It may come as a surprise to some parents that children are not born with the ability to listen, only with the ability to hear. It may also be surprising to them to learn that parents frequently don't know how to listen either. Even greater numbers of them don't know how to talk to their children in understandable language.

Persistent unacceptable behavior nearly always has its roots in poor listening; a result of the abstract and confusing messages parents unintentionally use in giving direction to their children and in expressing their parental prerogatives. "Don't dilly-dally," means nothing to the average five or six year old, nor does, "Be good!"

On the other hand, when little Cindy complains to mother that "Nobody loves me," too often mother doesn't understand that the real message is something else entirely.

The process of learning to listen begins at birth. It

1

doesn't happen automatically, but must be nurtured. This book shows how to do that and in the process eliminate or substantially reduce discipline problems. The approach is a straightforward, practical one.

This is not a "course," that is, one need not read the entire book before being able to put the principles contained in it into action. Instead, each chapter is designed to stand alone. The more chapters you read, of course, the more you will learn about how to get your child to listen. But in each chapter you will find valuable information to assist you in becoming more effective in getting your child to behave as you desire.

Even if your child is already a teenager, don't despair. You will learn in these pages how to communicate so that he will learn to listen to you—and you to him—in such a way that everybody wins.

Chapter 1

"You don't say"

"SOMETIMES I think Michael doesn't understand a word I say."

Does that have a familiar ring? If it does, you could be nearer the truth than you realize. If you seem to be having trouble getting your messages across to your child, maybe it's not his fault.

It's easy to forget that for children, especially those in their early years, the adult world is a perplexing one which seems to turn on an axis made of words; words which for the most part are strange to them. As if that wasn't bad enough, it often seems as though children are expected to be mind-readers, riddle-solvers, magicians and junior grade psychoanalysts.

As a first step in learning how to get your child to listen to you, we'll take a look at the kinds of communication errors which make it impossible for children to listen because the language used results in messages which are neither clear nor understandable to them. We'll begin with the worst offender.

THE ABSTRACTION

A week or so ago I was browsing in a bookstore. Nearby a young woman was searching the shelves, apparently trying to find a particular book.

"Are you being careful?" I heard her say. I looked up from the copy of *Denmark on $10 a Day* to observe the object of her concern, a little girl no more than three or three and a half years of age.

"Yes, mommy."

The tiny child was perched on one of those platform ladders that are scattered about the walls of bookstores. From her unsteady position she was busily rearranging all the carefully shelved volumes she could reach.

"That's a good girl." Without looking at her daughter, mother continued her hunt for the book she wanted. The bookstore owner's ulcer gained a bit.

I wondered what message this youthful mother wanted to convey to her daughter, and further, what message did the child receive? What was she responding to when she answered, "Yes, mommy?"

My experience in child psychology told me that three or three and a half year olds don't have the ability to deal with such abstractions as "being" and "careful." So whatever her wishes were, mommy was mistaken if she thought that she had communicated them to her daughter. Of course she was equally mistaken if she thought her daughter's response was an indication the child had understood the message.

Rule number one in the listening-communicating-game is that the *message sent isn't necessarily the message received.* One way adults ignore that rule when they talk with or to children is the use of words which are too abstract for children to understand. Here are some other anecdotes which are typical examples of how abstractions can backfire:

Carl was a kindergartener who was considered a menace by teachers and other children. He had a nasty habit of hitting his schoolmates, of either sex, with little or no provocation. In due course his parents were summoned by the school principal. Something would have to be done to stop this behavior, they were told, or Carl could not stay in school.

The boy's father was embarrassed and in his embarrassment he became angry.

"I'll take care of this and you can bet I'll put a stop to it!"

On arrival home, I learned later, the miniscule monster was subjected to a twenty- or thirty-minute lecture on the evils of hitting and how it was the pathway to a life of hardened criminality. The lad stopped listening about ten words into the discourse.

No longer after the sermon than the following morning, Carl again was sent to the principal's office. He had nearly annihilated another boy who had done nothing more than accidentally bump into him.

This was where I entered the picture. When the principal once more got in touch with Carl's parents, she suggested asking the psychologist to help. The now nearly desperate parents readily agreed.

"I don't know what else to do. I gave him a good talking-to yesterday, but he just doesn't listen!" complained father.

When I saw Carl, and after we were comfortable with one another, I broached the question of his father's instruction about the hitting.

"Carl, what did you do that you were sent to the office?"

"I hit David."

"But didn't your father tell you yesterday that you were not to hit other boys and girls?"

"Nope."

"What did he tell you?"

"He said I should be have (pronounced 'hayve') and I'm being have."

The admonition "behave" was as meaningless to Carl as the concept "careful" to the little girl in the bookstore.

In the next chapter we'll discuss the work of Jean Piaget. The renowned Swiss psychologist has shown that the ability to comprehend abstractions develops gradually. In the beginning, children deal in concrete words. If we attempt to communicate at a level which is beyond their listening ability, our messages will not be understood. That's not a simple thing to remember and it's much *less* simple to keep our messages on a concrete level. But if we make the child a partner in the process, we can be reasonably sure that we are sending messages which are within the bounds of his listening ability. In a later chapter we will discuss at length how to make the child a partner. For now what we should keep in mind is that we can't assume a child understands words just because they seem "simple" to us.

On one of the most widely used IQ tests there is an item which asks, "In what way are a cat and a mouse the same or alike?" The acceptable responses include something to the effect that they're both animals, both have tails, eyes, four feet, etc. That sounds easy enough, doesn't it? But the concept "same" and the concept "different" are abstractions and for many children, even well into the primary grades, they are beyond their listening ability. A colleague reported the following interaction with a kindergartener with regard to that particular item.

"In what way are a cat and a mouse the same or alike?"

"They're not."

"They're not?"

"Uh-uh. The cat's the same, but the mouse is different."

It's clear that the "same-different" classification was over the head of that youngster.

Another kind of question which is included in the same IQ test requires the child to tell what's missing from pictures of familiar objects. For example there's a comb with a couple of teeth broken off, simple enough, one might think. But the concept of "What's there-what's missing" is also difficult for many children and can also evoke some interesting responses. Another of the pictures shows a table with a leg missing. When I presented it to one first grader, he gazed at it carefully for a moment and then said, with absolute certainty,

"*Everything's* missing from that picture!"

True enough. There was no table cloth. There were no dishes or utensils, no people, nothing to indicate walls or a floor, etc., etc. Indeed, everything *was* missing.

Don't get the idea that only little ones are confused by language. One sixth grader had difficulty with another of the questions on the IQ test. The item asks the child to name the four seasons. This youngster replied, "Salt, pepper, mustard and vinegar."

An adult should never assume that his messages are clear to children. To give you an idea of what can happen, here are responses to test questions which were collected over a fifteen-year period by an anonymous teacher. They may be humorous to you, but to their writers they were an accurate reflection of the information to which they had been exposed, either in textbooks or through teacher's lectures. Their unintentional humor pervades many areas of learning.

For example here are some definitions:

- Strategy is when you don't let the enemy know you are out of ammunition, but keep on firing.
- By syntax is meant all the money collected by the Catholic Church from sinners.
- A virgin forest is a forest in which the hand of man has never set foot.

The humor is the result of combining accurate facts in an illogical sequence or of simple misunderstanding of the what the words mean.

On the subject of geography the children had these ideas:

- The general direction of the Alps is straight up.
- Most of the houses of France are made of Plaster of Paris.
- Manhatten Island was bought from the Indians for $24, and I do not believe you could buy it now for $500.
- New Zealand is a democratic country. They passed a law there preventing women from sweating in the factories.
- The climate is hottest next to the Creator.

Those are examples of communication rule 1: *The message sent is not necessarily the message received.* In two of the responses, the humor is the result of supplying more information than was asked for.

History too received humorous treatment at the hands of the sixth graders, as witness these examples:

- If it hadn't been for Greece, we wouldn't have any history.
- The Pope declared Luther's writing to be hereditary.
- The French Revolution was caused by overcharging taxis.
- Napoleon wanted an heir to the throne, but since Josephine was a baroness, she could not bear children.
- Henry VIII, by his own efforts, increased the population of England by 40,000.
- Queen Elizabeth was a fat woman. The demands of the Spanish Ambassador she stoutly resisted.
- Oliver Cromwell had a large red nose, but under it were deeply religious feelings.
- He fought the battle of Worcester on the anniversary of his death.
- When a Northern soldier could not go to war, he sent a prostitute.
- What was the cause of the Industrial Revolution? Ans. People stopped reproducing by hand and started reproducing by machinery.
- The Civil War was started by Lincoln singing the Emanculation Proculmation.

Hard as it may be for parents to believe, those bits of information were precisely what the children *thought* they had read or been told by their teacher. They're just close enough to the facts to be almost credible when read superficially.

The greatest skill of communication is the ability to write—to produce literature correct in form and style and comprehensible. A lot of study is required before one can produce literature, but as we've seen, not all study produces accurate learning. Here are some further examples of the way sixth graders go astray:

- What kind of a noun is trousers? Ans. An uncommon noun because it is singular on top and plural at the bottom.
- Name three relative pronouns. Ans. Aunt, uncle and brother.
- A scout obeys all to whom obedience is due and respects all duly constipated authorities.
- Animal husbandry is the act of having more than one husband.
- As she is going to be married next month, she is busy getting her torso ready.
- The men who followed Jesus around were called the twelve opposums.
- Mrs. Smith has given $10,000 to build a home for indignant women.

General science and human physiology were also challenged and vanquished by the sixth grade scholars, to wit, the following:

- Why do we not raise silk worms in the U.S.? Ans. We get our silk from rayon. He is a larger animal and gives more silk.
- The dinosaur became extinct after the flood because they were too big to get in the ark.
- One by-product of cattle raising is calves.
- How is bacteria reproduced? Ans. They multiply and then divide.
- In the spring, the salmon ascends the fresh-water streams to spoon.
- The moon is a planet just like the earth, only deader.
- What happens when there is an eclipse of the sun? Ans. A great many people come out to look at it.
- The triangle which has an angle of 135 degrees is called an obscene triangle.
- Describe the circulation of the blood. Ans. It flows down one leg and up the other.
- The spinal column is a long bunch of bones. The head sits on top and you sit on the bottom.

- To prevent head colds, use an agonizer to spray nose until it drops into your throat.
- A person should take a bath once in the summer time and not so often in the winter.
- The stomach is a bowl-shaped cavity containing the organs of indigestion.

Finally, and fittingly, government received its fair share of student "bafflegab." Turn about is, after all, fair play.

- The difference between a president and a king is that a king has no vice.
- Tell how a city purifies its water. Ans. They filter the water and then force it through an aviator.
- The limited monarchy—Only one man can be king at a time.

It may or may not be important for children to be able to answer questions on an IQ test correctly or to parrot back information learned by rote. It *is* important that children be able to listen to and respond properly to the instructions of their parents. For that to happen the instructions must be expressed in words the children can understand and mother and dad must make sure they were understood.

Children are not born with the ability to listen—only with the ability to hear, which is something vastly different. Unfortunately, listening is a skill which is generally not taught at home, and from my observation is certainly not taught in school. Without intending to confuse, most parents and teachers nevertheless use words which are vague and misleading to children and provide confusing cues.

The Miscue

Miscue words often are the subject of humor such as the story in which a man who had never heard of

Rudyard Kipling was asked, "Do you like Kipling?" "I don't know," he replied, "I've never kippled."

But miscue words can also lead to frustration as happened with Melissa's mother, who was at her wit's end. Melissa was habitually late for school. Her mother repeatedly admonished her second grade daughter. "If you didn't dawdle in the bathroom every morning, you'd have plenty of time to get to school."

Each time Melissa would promise not to "dawdle." But she continued to be tardy. Teacher suggested that the psychologist might be able to help. I spoke with the girl's mother first and she told me about Melissa's dawdling.

When I talked with the child, on a hunch I asked her if she had really stopped dawding. She was indignant.

"I promised mommy I wouldn't dawdle, and I don't dawdle!"

"What does dawdle mean, Melissa?"

"I don't know, but I know I don't do it!"

We have seen that children can't be taught how to listen if the messages they are given by mother and dad are so abstract as to be incomprehensible to them. If abstractions were the only problem, it would seem that an easy remedy would be to make certain only concrete words are used. But parents include other kinds of traps in their communication, even without speaking.

The Unintentional Message

Novelist Ayn Rand believes that it's hard to do good without doing harm. Her idea was certainly true as far as one young mother was concerned.

About a month ago I received a phone call from the principal of a primary grade school.

"Could you come in and talk with one of my classroom aides? I think she needs some help, judging from what the teacher of the class tells me."

"I'd be glad to, but fill me in. What seems to be the problem?"

"I don't know, really, except that the aide says she's having all kinds of trouble with her little girl. The teacher sees that there's something wrong, too, and she recommended that her aide talk with you."

I assured the principal that I would be glad to talk with the aide and set up an appointment to visit her at the school.

She turned out to be a very young woman, very intelligent and very much of the "now" generation.

"I never realized what a can of worms I was opening when I became a school aide," she began.

"How do you mean?"

"Well, I think my problems with Lisa—my daughter—have something to do with my working in her kindergarten room."

"Problems?"

"Yes. I don't know why, but Lisa simply refuses to do any work; or anything else, for that matter. I'd quit, or ask for a transfer to another room, but I feel I have a commitment to this particular group of kids now. I want to see it through until the end of the year. It's like I have a stake in their future."

"What does Lisa do?"

"Like I said, nothing. She just sits. And when I try to get her to do what the others are doing, she just turns away from me."

"Um hm."

"It really hurts. I just don't know how to handle this. I mean if she had a father, I would at least have someone to help me. But my husband left us. He's living somewhere in Southern California and he's remarried. He couldn't care less anyway. That's probably why Lisa is the way she is—just like her father."

"Then you've had other difficulties with Lisa before this?"

"No. It was unfair of me to say that. Lisa is really a sweet child. It's just that she has really hurt me. We've gotten along just great up until now. She's very bright and she can even write her name and read and we used to have marvelous conversations. Would you believe she's really into medicine?"

"Medicine?"

"Uh huh, I just completed my pre–med work. I guess with all the books lying around, Lisa got interested."

"You plan to become a physician?"

"Well, I did, but now I'm not sure. I really dig working with kids. Maybe I should be a teacher."

"In spite of your present troubles with Lisa?"

"Oh, sure. It isn't the whole class, you know, it's just Lisa I'm having the problem with. The rest of the kids seem to love me and I love them."

"They show their affection for you?"

"Yes, they hang onto my hands and my skirt–you know."

"And you show your affection for them?"

"It would be hard not to."

"Does Lisa join the group of hangers-on?"

"No, she won't come anywhere near me, just wanders off and pouts and won't have any part of it."

"Any part of your affection?"

"Uh, yes, I guess maybe that's it, but I never thought of it that way. It seems different when you put it like that."

"How do you mean?"

"Well, like I'm only giving her a share of my love."

"Do you think she might feel that way?"

"I hadn't thought about it until now, but maybe she does. You know, come to think of it, that might be exactly the problem."

It was obvious that the young mother had had what psychotherapists call an "Ah Hah! experience." Her newly gained insight was the first step in the resolution of her difficulties with Lisa. But it was Lisa who actually provided the answer.

Matters were brought sharply into focus when I brought the little girl into the office to talk with her mother while I sat in to facilitate communication. As it turned out, my help in that regard was unnecessary.

I'm a familiar figure in the school and in the classrooms, so an introduction to Lisa wasn't needed. I did explain to her that I was there to help her mother with her work in the classroom and that we needed Lisa's help, too. She said nothing and turned her face toward the wall. After half a minute or so, her mother said,

"Lisa, I just don't know why you aren't doing anything in class and neither does your teacher. Don't you want to get good marks?"

"I can't do that stuff. It's too hard. And anyway, I don't care!"

"But Lisa, you *can* do the work. And if you can't, I'll help you just like I help all the other children."

At that point Lisa burst into tears.

"But you're *my* mommy," she sobbed.

There it was, as clear and concise as only a child could put it. Lisa's mother was crying now, too, as she understood how she had hurt her little girl.

Later she told me that now she realized that she had gone out of her way not to give Lisa any special attention. If Lisa raised her hand to answer a question, she would never be called on first. Other children were always given help with their work before Lisa was. And Lisa would have to compete for her mother's hand to hang on to at recess time. Generally she would not even comment on Lisa's neat papers or other praiseworthy work, but would go out of her way to compliment the work of the other children. What she didn't realize was that Lisa was getting a message that was sent unintentionally.

Fortunately this case had a happy ending. Because the teacher saw that her aide might be causing a problem for her child in some way, she sought help in defining the problem and was able to help Lisa's mother carry through a plan to correct it. Lisa, her mother and the teacher are now doing very nicely and all have a much better understanding of their own and each other's needs than they had before.

And there's another communication rule to be learned from that story: One cannot *not* communicate.

THE SHORT-CIRCUIT

On a recent trip, as I was nearing the hotel elevator, I saw that the doorway was partially blocked by a young man about eleven or twelve years old. The boy was actually pressing on the rubber boot at the edge of the door to hold it open. Whether for me, or because he was fascinated by the mechanism, I couldn't tell. Whatever the reason, his action angered his father, who grabbed him by the arm and pulled him toward the rear of the car. Through gritted teeth he hissed,

"How many times have I told you not to stand in the door of the elevator?"

There was no answer, so the question was repeated, with a little more anger the second time.

"How many times have I told you not to stand in the door of the elevator?"

Silence tinged with embarrassment (the boy's, the father's—and mine.)

"Answer me! How many times?"

Mercifully at that point the elevator reached the lobby. As I walked away, I could hear the father continuing to try to extract a number from his son. It was almost a game. I imagined the boy replying,

"Eight times?"

And the father saying gleefully,

"Wrong! Try another number."

I assumed that what this father was trying to accomplish was to get his son not to block the doorway of the elevator. I wondered whether it would have been more effective for him to show the boy that he could press the "Open Door" button on the control panel if he wanted to keep the door open. As for how many times he had told the youngster "not to stand in the doorway of the elevator," I wondered about that too. I had an idea that what he actually said was something more like, "I'm sick and tired of telling you things and being ignored!" This was a case of a child "failing to listen" not because his father's words were abstract, but because they missed the mark completely—they short-circuited.

The greatest danger of the short-circuit is that it invites the user to become sarcastic. For example, suppose mother has been waging a battle to get her daughter to "straighten up" her room (that's another common abstraction.) After three weeks of constant bickering, mother walks in one day and lo and behold! The room is neat and tidy. What she would like her daughter to know is something like, "I'm pleased that you cleaned your room, it looks beautiful." Instead she becomes trapped in a short-circuit and her message becomes, "Well, I see you've finally cleaned up the mess. I didn't think I'd live long enough to see it happen!" With that kind of sarcastic reward, chances are pretty fair that it won't happen again. At least not without another lengthy battle.

THE IMPOSSIBLE DEMAND

Another frequent cause of listening failure is the kind of message which sets up a condition the child can't possibly meet. I heard an impossible demand not too long ago in a supermarket. Let me preface the incident with the observation that I'm convinced that mothers who take toddlers to the supermarket must have no other place to leave them—either that or they have masochistic tendencies and enjoy suffering. From what I've witnessed, it's usually a harrowing experience for mother, for the poor clerk who has to re-stack the boxes and cans in those displays which little ones find so irresistible, and in the end, if you'll pardon the pun, it's painful for the child in most cases.

Now, as to the impossible demand I heard in the supermarket. It came as the culmination of the following scene: A little boy about six years of age was dashing madly through the aisles with mother close behind. On the straightaway mommy was no match for him, but as he rounded a turn, his undeveloped coordination cost him just enough speed so that mother was able to grasp him. He was held fast by one arm and simultaneously whacked so soundly on the bottom that both feet came off the floor. I couldn't hear all of mother's words because by this time the boy was displaying the full range and pitch of his voice, screaming "No, I don't want to!" I did hear, in a loud voice, the command, "I told you to stop that crying and act your age! Now stop crying!" The words were accompanied by another solid whack on the behind.

Talk about an impossible demand. The frustrated mother wanted her six-year-old to stop crying immediately, even as she was spanking him. As for "acting his age," judging from his apparent unwillingness to obey, he was acting in a manner that's typical of six-year-olds.

THE DOUBLE-WHAMMY

This is a cross between the short circuit and the impossible demand. One of the most frequently used is something like,

"Just who do you think you are, young man?"

This is a short-circuited message because it doesn't really ask what mother or father wants to know—at least I don't think it does. It certainly won't accomplish whatever is desired of the child. For example, if he has just "talked back" to his mother, it's doubtful that junior's assessment of who he is will alter his behavior in the future.

An automobile commercial which is being seen on TV and being heard on radio as of the writing of this chapter claims that the sponsor's product is, "the car for the man who knows who he is." As many times as I have seen and heard those words, I am still unable to determine how knowing who one is becomes a criterion for selecting a car—or anything else.

Another commercial pokes fun at that one. It presents an elegant gentleman with a Spanish accent who claims that *his* product is, "the car for the man who knows who I am." The parody makes about as much sense as the original and it's humorous.

To ask a child, "Who do you think you are?" is, as we said, an impossible demand. Don't expect an answer unless you have a budding philosopher for a son or daughter. Try the question on yourself, as a matter of fact. I'd give odds that you respond by giving your name or your occupation, neither of which, I suspect, is going to tell who you really think you are.

THE JUNIOR PSYCHOANALYST

This is a very popular message classification with parents. The junior psychoanalyst type message begins with the question, "Why?"

"Why did you do that?"

"Why did you hit your sister?"

"Why did you take the money from my purse?"

Junior psychoanalyst or "why?" messages are related to abstractions and, distantly, to impossible demands. What is the meaning of "why"? This kind of message assumes that the child has the ability to do an instant self-analysis and come up with a reason which somehow apparently will excuse the behavior. As long as junior knows *why* he did the deed, it's OK. But actually mother and dad aren't so much interested in why the behavior occurred as in preventing it's occurrence in the future.

The use of the correct alternative to the junior psychoanalyst or why message is an easy habit to acquire because it gets an immediate response in almost all cases. Next time your child behaves in a manner you find unacceptable, preface your question with "what?" rather than "why?" No matter what the offense, ask,

"What did you do?"

If money was taken from mother's purse, the question is still, "What did you do?" The chances are you'll get a reply something like,

"I took some money from mommy's purse."

If you don't get such a response, tell the child what he did: "You took money from mother's purse."

This has the effect of concentrating on the behavior itself. It draws the child's attention to his misdeed. What was done is concrete and can be dealt with. Why it was done may be abstract and the child can't deal with it, nor can you.

There's more to the use of "what" questions than this brief coverage tells and we'll talk more about the technique later in the book. For now it's sufficient that you remember to avoid junior psychoanalyst or "why" questions.

The Threat

Threats are to be avoided at all costs. They're far too dangerous to use.

"If you do that just once more, I'll . . ."

That becomes an invitation to the child to do whatever it is once more. Isn't that what mommy or daddy said to do?

"If you don't stop this instant, you're going to get it!"

Oh goody, a surprise! I wonder what I'm going to get, little Betsy ponders. Only way to find out is to keep on doing whatever elicited the promise.

"OK, now you've done it. Just wait until your father gets home!"

How's that for setting up dear old dad as the family ogre? The poor man has been gone all day and his first act when he walks into the house will be to punish his child—for an offense he didn't even witness.

"I'm warning you!"

Most often those words are not followed by a statement of the consequence—or an alternative, so they're meaningless to the child. "You're warning me *what*?"

"Just never mind!"

There are other typical kinds of threats, of course. What's dangerous about all of them is that either they're not enforced, there's no consequence, or if they are enforced, the cost is much too high. For example,

"If you do that once more, you're never going to come to the store with me again!"

That means (a) mother has to go to the store in the evening—or whenever dad's home to babysit, (b) she has to hire a babysitter, (c) grandma gets stuck with the chore or (d) she'll have to hire a professional shopper.

In Chapter One we learned that children's misbehaviors are the result of listening failure and that listening failure is caused by parental messages which are unclear or incomprehensible to the child. Major message errors are (1) Abstractions, (2) Miscues, (3) The Unintentional Message, (4) Short-Circuits, (5) Impossible Demands, (6) Double-Whammies, (7) Junior Psychoanalyst or "why" questions and (8) Threats.

While this first chapter may appear simple, the reader is advised to go over it again with an eye and an ear to becoming aware of his own message patterns. Generally parents will habitually use one or more of these kinds of messages when talking to or attempting to discipline their children. They are so stereotyped in each of us that if we examine our messages for a few days we can quickly identify those we are accustomed to using. Once identified, they can be corrected.

Before we leave this chapter, I want to direct your attention to the other side of the communication process. Obviously, no matter how careful you are to make your messages concrete and so on, you can't communicate effectively with your child if he doesn't know how to listen.

In Appendix A I have listed a number of exercises you can do with your child to improve his ability to listen. I strongly recommend that these be used with small children.

In Chapter Two we're going to look at some of the more intriguing aspects of speech development. The information will provide you with greater insight into your child's listening capacities at various ages. You may find that you have been expecting too much too soon.

Chapter 2

Out of the Mouths of Babes

WHEN I say that babies can communicate I expect a lot of arguments. That's only natural; think of the word "communicate," and you immediately get the idea it means the use of words—talking and listening. But when you stop to think about it a bit more, you know it's entirely possible to communicate without talking in the usual sense.

Those who are seriously hearing-impaired, for example, communicate through sign language. Your dog or cat has learned to communicate so well that it has trained you to recognize that when it gives certain signals, it wants to enter or leave the house or be fed.

You know when someone is angry or upset because that message is communicated to you through what's called "body language." Babies "communicate" in the same kinds of ways, without spoken language, from the time of birth.

No mother needs reminding that her baby's first communications were closely linked to her care and nurturing. Almost always (maybe I should delete the "almost") when her baby cries, mother will have some kind of chore to take care of.

When he was hardly more than a baby himself, my younger son once observed, "Babies aren't really good for much. They just lie around and sleep and eat and cry and mess their diapers." I'm not sure he had the sequence just right, but he was doing a good job of describing how babies communicate.

When mother responds by changing his diaper, she has acknowledged that her baby has communicated with her. But baby doesn't know that his mother's response to his cry is a communication. That's an important consideration. That kind of communication, because it's one way, isn't really communication at all.

For true communication to take place, each party has to be aware not only that the other is trying to communicate, but also that his idea of what the communication means isn't necessarily shared by the other. In the case of baby's cries, for example, mother might assume the baby's message is that he's wet. But she isn't really sure, until she actually investigates, why her baby is crying. He could be wet, hungry, sleepy, colicky, or he might just want to be held.

We'll talk more about one-way communication later on. Right now, let's look at the way baby's ability to communicate develops. We need to know more about the stages of language development so that we won't demand more listening ability of children than their level of development—their language sophistication—will allow.

In our discussion of language development, we'll draw on the theories of experts in the comparatively new field called "psycholinguistics." Don't let that word frighten you. It simply means the application of psychological theory to the study of language. We'll also talk about the work of Swiss psychologist Jean Piaget, who derived a lot of his theories from the observation of his own children.

During the first period of his life, your baby is completely egocentric. He's sure he himself is real, but he's not so sure about the world. He has the impression that it's not really permanent. It's unlikely that even the most diligent student of babyhood would presume to say that he knows exactly how an infant sees the world, but observation and experience have provided some clues. Baby's world has been described as something like dreaming that you're watching a magician make something disappear and you believe that it really has ceased to exist.

During this first period of his life, your baby begins to lay the foundation for learning language. He makes the kinds of sounds all babies do. At this stage the sounds are only random.

Parents of three month old babies are elated when they first hear a clearly pronounced "dadada" and they're sure that their baby has spoken his first word. Unfortunately all that has happened is that baby has found a way to make sounds that amuse him and evoke smiles and other rewards from his parents. Nevertheless, these are the kinds of sounds which he will later put together to make words and sentences. These "cooing" kinds of noises your baby makes are called "phonemes." In adult American speech there are about forty-five of these phonemes. By the time he has reached the age of eight to ten months, a baby is able to produce about one third of that number.

Also, at about the eighth to tenth month, your baby's idea of the kind of place the world is has changed. He now sees it as more permanent and the things in it as more constant. Now, should a magician pretend to make something disappear, the baby would look for it. He has progressed from an awareness of his world as a here and now one, to one that also includes the not here and the not now. This change in his view of the world is most important to language development, because the process called "labeling" can now take place. We'll talk more about that a little later.

In spite of this growth, your baby at this stage still has an egocentric view of the environment. For example, it isn't objects themselves that have permanence, but his actions in relation to them. If you approach him and present a toy, and then hide the toy behind a newspaper to the baby's right, he will look for it there and find it. If you then hide the toy behind the paper to the baby's left, he will still search for it on the right because when he did so the first time, he was successful.

It's during this same period of development that your baby displays body language which signals that he now views the world as permanent. One of Piaget's children, as he was watching her play one day, provided an example of this.

The child was accustomed to sucking her thumb just before going to sleep each night. On one occasion during the daytime, as she was playing with her pillow, she began to suck on its fringe. As she did, she lay down and curled up as if sleeping. After about thirty seconds, she got up and resumed playing.

Piaget surmised that the action of sucking combined with the pillow reminded the child of her sleep routine. Here was evidence that the concept of sleep was not only a here and now thing; it also existed at another time and another place.

Other gestural signals your baby uses at this time are facial expressions—smiles and frowns, for example—and vocal utterances which are designed actually to identify things. One of my own children, at about ten months of age, used the utterance "kaidn" to represent milk.

With the beginning of this kind of body and vocal signaling, your baby's world becomes a social one. No longer is it merely a physical one. Now there's a need to have around him others who can use the same kinds of signals and thus communicate with him. Meanwhile, his store of phonemes increases.

By the time he's a year old, the average baby uses eighteen phonemes, almost half the number used by the average adult American. Something else is also taking place. Baby's phonemes gradually come to resemble the phonemes used by adults in his own nation and culture.

It's fascinating to note that in all countries and all cultures, babies at first utter the same sounds. The gutteral and nasal sounds of French and the difficult German vowel sounds come naturally to American babies. But if you have studied either of these languages as an adult, you know how hard it is to produce those sounds. What happens is that since they don't occur in English, babies neither hear adults making them, nor are they rewarded for making them. Gradually the ability to produce the sounds disappears.

Although it's a widely held belief that babies learn language by imitating their parents, that isn't entirely true. The sequence is more like this: Baby hears his parents make sounds that he has already produced spontaneously. He limits his production to these familiar sounds rather than mimicking unfamiliar, new ones.

As he develops, baby does, by imitation, select combinations of familiar sounds he hears adults producing. He then uses these combinations when there is a repetition of the situation which occurred the first time he heard them.

As an example, let's assume that baby spontaneously produced the phonemes which make up the word "dog." If he hears that combination of sounds used by his mother whenever the family pet enters the room, he will produce the combination in imitation when the dog enters the room. But the association is with the situation, not the dog. We'll get to that in just a moment.

Just why babies are motivated to imitate adult speech isn't completely clear. One possibility is that imitation persists because it produces satisfying consequences for baby, such as mother's attention, a hug, or a smile from daddy.

Another possibility may be that the baby associates the sounds with mother's attention or daddy's smile. Thus, when he produces the imitative sounds, he re-experiences those pleasant events.

Whatever the motivation, by the time he reaches his first birthday, baby has learned to make meaningful associations between words and what they represent. The term often used is "labeling." For example, the relationship between the phonemes which make up the spoken word, "door," and the opening through which one passes from room to room becomes clear. The child now places the label, "door" on the proper object in his environment.

This is a significant step along the pathway toward the acquisition of language. But there is still some distance to go before the child is able to use symbolic social communication. His "language" is still largely confined to pointing at objects, rather than utterances of the symbols—words—which represent them.

At the one year mark, baby still can't be credited with using language. His utterances are usually limited to two, or at the most, three sounds of one syllable or a duplicated syllable. Most frequently one hears "dada" or "mama." But this is another big step, because "dada" is more than just a spontaneous utterance or an imitation of particular sounds heard in a particular situation. "Dada" is now meant by the child to be a communication. It can mean, "Where's daddy," "I want my daddy," "Daddy, stop that," or anything else the baby may want to communicate with respect to his father. But still the child is not using true language. More development must take place before that happens.

The development of language varies greatly from child to child. In part this is caused by variations in the rate of maturation, but it's also the result of the child's experiences with language in his environment. Infants who are talked to and rewarded by their parents for making sounds will produce more sounds as a result.

Psychologists have found evidence which strongly supports the idea that children who have many language experiences tend to grow up more emotionally healthy and more able to deal with social situations than those who don't. One study showed the importance of exposure to and involvement in language during the first fifteen months of life.

Researchers found that the amount of language directed at the twelve to fifteen-month-old by his parents, by television, conversation, etc., was a key factor in development. The more of such language exposure during that period, the better the child's social learning skills at age two and age three. There was also greater psychological well-being.

Further, children who were developing well socially and psychologically at age three were also better adjusted at age six. There seems to be substantial evidence that one of the best things you can do for your child is to encourage speech development beginning at birth.

We referred earlier to the use of one word utterances. It was pointed out that these do not deserve the term "language." In the true sense, the use of one word utterances to convey a message is not language. Language implies the ability to put words together in sequences which communicate complex messages directly. When your child truly uses language, you don't have to infer the message from the situation in which it was delivered.

An example of the difference is the illustration used earlier of the baby's single word utterance, "dada." As we pointed out, that could mean, "Daddy's home," "Where's Daddy," or "Daddy's a funny man." Only the situation in which the baby said "dada" tells his parents just what he is trying to say. If the word occurs just as daddy enters the house, his parents can infer it means "Daddy's home." If it occurs when daddy goes to work in the morning, his parents might infer that "dada" means "Where's daddy?" or "Daddy's gone."

On the other hand, when the baby learns to string two words together, his language can be used to convey more complex messages. He can now say, "Where daddy?" or "Daddy allgone."

This stringing together of words isn't a haphazard thing. It has to be done according to a set of rules—a system, and it's an active process. Although the one-year-old who is able to utter only one word at a time may very well have a system for understanding a wide variety of grammatical patterns, he does not yet have an *active* system. Such a system would require the combining of words into sentences.

The next big jump in language acquisition takes place at about one and a half years of age. At that point the child begins putting together two-word sentences. From this beginning, language development is rapid, although as we stated, greatly different with each child. In a seven month period, one child's two-word sentences increased two hundred fold, from 14 to 2500.

There is a definite structure to these two-word sentences. They are typically made up of two classes of words, which language experts call "pivot" and "open class." Parents are familiar with the pivot word "allgone;" pivot, because many other words can be attached to it to make sentences. "Milk allgone," "Doggie allgone," etc. Open class words can precede or follow pivot words, that is "Allgone milk," or "Milk allgone." Another pivot word frequently used is "where"; "Where house?" "Where toy?" etc.

An important point to remember about the child's language structure at this stage is that as far as he's concerned it employs only the two kinds of words listed: pivot and open class. Even more important is the fact that the grammatical structure of the child does not necessarily agree with adult grammatical structure. The reason adults can talk to small children in spite of this difference is that adults have learned "social speech," which is simply another way of saying that adults are able, to some extent at least, to fit the words to the audience. Children are not able to do this.

Not all adults use social speech in talking to children. The chances are that if you felt a need to read this book, either you don't use social speech with your child or you don't use it to a sufficient degree. One of the main things you'll learn in these pages is how to use your adult knowledge of your child's perspective to get him to listen to your messages. Right now, let's talk a little about social speech.

In one study, a series of experiments in communication were run in which two persons were separated by a partition. Each of them had a sheet of paper before him which contained the same six designs. The designs were nonstandard geometric shapes so constructed that they couldn't be identified as simply "triangle," "parallelogram," etc. One of the pair had to describe each design to the other who would then put an identifying number on it.

Adult subjects made few errors, even when the initial careful description was reduced. As the experiment was repeated, the subjects arrived at an agreed upon social code. For example, after the third trial, the description might have been something such as "scalloped edges." By the fourth trial the person who was supposed to identify the design could do so with only a one-word description, e.g. "scalloped." Since the word grew out of the social process set up in the experiment, however, the one word description would have been relatively meaningless to someone who had not participated in it.

When typical adult descriptions were communicated to children in a similar experiment, not one of the children made any errors in identifying the designs, even when the descriptions were shortened. But when children were asked to describe the designs to each other, they were unable to communicate them. Instead of careful description, they gave the designs names which were based solely on their own individual perspectives. For example, the "scalloped edge" design might have been named "Kitty," for some reason known only to that particular child.

Surprisingly, at the fifth grade level, children were no better than kindergarteners on the first trial and improved only slowly with successive trials. Ninth grade children made great improvement after several trials, but still did not do as well as adults did from the outset.

The message you should take from this is that even by the time he is in fifth grade, your child still does not have social language. He is still not able to fit his communication to the audience; you, for instance. In ninth grade there is still some need for improvement before his social language is equal to yours.

But let's get back to the language development of the child where we left off: at eighteen months of age. Just how subject to verbal control is his behavior at that point? As we saw, this is a period of rapid growth in language acquisition. Some children develop a repertoire of as many as 2500 or more two-word utterances during the ensuing seven month period.

At around two years of age another major milestone is reached: verbs are used to construct three-word sentences. Children at that age have been observed to utter a two-word combination such as "Want milk," and follow immediately with "Robert want milk." That's a long jump from "Want milk."

The use of verbs is important. As the child acquires more and more language, his motor behavior—his actions—are more and more subject to control by the language of his parents and other adults. Most parents begin their attempts at such control with the familiar "No, no!" when the child acts in a way which is not acceptable. They soon learn that this command is ineffective. They simply can't keep up with the investigatory activities of their child. It seems at times that everything is forbidden. There is a story about a boy who was supposedly fourteen before he realized his name wasn't "No, No, Bobby."

But with the advent of increased language ability, the child is not only controllable by the words of his parents, but by his own words. With the ability to "label" objects and actions and the events that stimulate the actions, the child is able to tell himself what to do or not do.

If you are the parent of an infant only a few months of age you should be aware that your verbal commands, e.g. "No, no," have no effect on the actions of your child. You would be much better off simply to put out of harm's way anything you would like to keep in one piece. If your child is in danger, or is about to perform an action toward another, physically removing him from the situation is the answer, not a verbal command.

By the time the child is a year and a half, perhaps a bit younger or older, depending on the child, he will at least give some response to show his awareness of verbal commands. For example, at this stage he will look at the person who gave the command and make a trial move to repeat whatever action seemed to have prompted it.

Even three- or four-year-old children cannot be expected to respond to verbal commands to discontinue an undesirable action once initiated. Nor can you expect that a command such as, "Put that down and play with this instead," will be obeyed. It's not that your child is wilfully disobedient; he just doesn't have sufficiently internalized language to mediate or govern his behavior. He can't tell himself to stop.

What you can expect of your three- or four-year-old is that he will respond to your command not to do something he is *about* to do. For example, if he's about to hit his baby brother, normally your command, "Robert, don't hit Billy!" will be obeyed. At least, as far as your child's language development is concerned, you have a right to expect it will be.

Because verbs are so important to your child's developing communication/listening ability, let's talk about them for a moment. An interesting observation of linguistic specialists is that irregular verbs are first learned correctly. It has been widely assumed that past tenses of irregular verbs are produced by children simply adding the "ed" to regular verbs. But according to psycholinguist Dan I. Slobin, "In all cases which have been studied, the first past tenses used are the correct forms of irregular verbs— 'came,' 'broke,' 'went,' and so on . . . Then, as soon as the child learns only one or two past tense forms—like 'helped' and 'walked'—he immediately replaces the correct irregular past tense forms with their incorrect overgeneralizations from the regular forms. Thus children say 'it came off,' 'it broke,' and 'he did it,' before they say 'it comed off,' 'it breaked,' and 'he doed it.' Even though the correct forms may have been practiced for several months they are driven out of the child's speech by the overregularization, and may not return for years."[1]

What's especially puzzling about that is the lack of a model to imitate. Obviously children don't hear their parents using incorrect past tenses of irregular verbs, and yet they persist. As Slobin says "One cannot help but be impressed with the child's great propensity to generalize, to analogize, to look for regularities—in short, to seek and create order in his language."[2]

Throughout the first four years of life, then, the child is engaged in building a means of communication—a language. By the time he's four, he's capable of following the instructions of adults, even fairly complicated ones. At first, children talk aloud to themselves as they use language to guide their actions. At around five, their speech becomes covert and they perform actions silently. It seems at times that their speech has disappeared. Occasionally, when children utter stray remarks, we can see that speech has not disappeared, but has only taken new concealed forms.

[1] Dan I. Slobin, *Psycholinguistics*, Illinois, Scott Foresman, 1971, p. 49.
[2] *Ibid.*, p. 50.

About mid-way through kindergarten another milestone is reached. From that point on, just about everything your child learns involves language. That's a most important thing for parents to know because it also includes behavior. If you want to teach your child to behave in certain ways, remember that behavior that is learned when the use of language is acquired quickly is highly stable and readily spreads to other activities. Those behaviors which are taught in the absence of language tend to be unstable, are quickly forgotten and must be constantly reinforced. Past five years of age, children control their behavior through internalized "verbal mediation." Let's talk about how that works and how you can use it to get your child to listen.

To begin with, note that in the final analysis, if he's going to do what you want, your child has to listen not to you, but to himself. Note also that you can't *make* him listen to you, but neither can he refuse to listen to himself. What you need to do then, is to see that what he hears from himself directs him to the kind of behavior that you—and, we'll assume, he—desire.

As we said, once your child has reached five years of age his language development has reached a point where his behavior is controlled by his thoughts. There are at least three ways to think. We can think with mental images, for example. It's said that Einstein developed his theories in that manner. Another way to think is with muscular movements. John Broadus Watson, the American behavioral psychologist, believed that thought was nothing more than covert movement of the small muscles of the throat. A third way of thinking is with words. It's this last way which is easiest to deal with.

We said earlier that in the final analysis, your child must learn to listen not to you but to himself in order for him to be able to control his behavior. If he has attained the developmental stage which will permit that, you can help him to gain self control by teaching him the skill of verbal mediation. In the following paragraphs, I'll tell you how to do that.

Verbal mediation is simply talking to one's self, and the process is just as simple as it is effective.

Misbehaviors are deviations from rules which you have established. First of all, your child must know what the rules are. We'll assume he does. If he then breaks the rules, it's because he has acted on impulse, not on the basis of thought. The impulsive child is seduced by the temptation which comes between him and the rule. But the child who is able to resist the temptation to break rules concentrates on his behavior and on what will happen to him if he gives in to temptation.

Verbal mediation is aimed at teaching the child to think of the consequences before he acts. This isn't a natural thing for a child to do. You must help him to see what the possible outcome will be if he breaks a rule. This doesn't mean that you threaten him. In chapter one we discussed the pitfalls of threats.

Unpleasant consequences may occur as a natural result of an action. For example, if your child refuses to get out of bed in the morning and is late for school, having to make excuses for himself in the school office may be sufficient to change his tardy behavior.

But sometimes unpleasant consequences don't occur naturally. For example, if your child eats candy you had bought for a card party (unless he eats so much that he becomes ill), there is no unpleasant consequence. In that case, you have to provide one. You might, for instance, make him pay for the candy out of his allowance. The kinds of unpleasant consequences you decide upon are up to you, but remember that the punishment should fit the crime. We'll talk more about that in Chapter Five.

Dr. Ralph Blackwood describes the process of mediation as one in which you change the emphasis from what *you* should say when your child misbehaves to training your child how to talk to *himself* about his behavior and its consequences. The training consists of teaching your child to ask himself, and to answer, four questions:

1. What did you do wrong?

2. What happens when you (name the misbehavior) that you don't like?
3. What should you have done instead?
4. What happens that you like when you (name the desired behavior)?[3]

Let's run through a hypothetical situation so you can see how this works. It's about four-thirty on a weekday afternoon. Your school age child is outside, playing with her friends. You want her to come in and get cleaned up for dinner. You go to the door and call,

"Janie, it's almost time to come in. I'll give you five minutes, then I'll call you and I want you to come." (You *should* give a warning, incidentally.)

"OK, mommy." (From her response you assume that Janie heard your message.)

Five minutes pass. As you promised, you go to the door and call Janie again. She acknowledges your call and you return to your dinner preparation. Fifteen minutes pass and you realize that Janie still hasn't come in. You call her once more.

"I don't want to come in yet."

You don't reply. Instead you walk to where Janie is and say calmly but firmly, "I want you to come in immediately." Unless Janie is completely incorrigible, she'll obey your order.

Let's assume that this kind of behavior is habitual with Janie. Here's how mediation training is done:

After Janie has gotten herself cleaned up and you have simmered down, you say,

"Janie, from now on I want you to come in when I call you. I don't like it when you refuse to come in. This afternoon you were fifteen minutes late. Because you did not come in until fifteen minutes after I called, tonight I am going to turn off your favorite television program fifteen minutes early." (Or whatever appropriate consequence you select.)

You can expect protests—ignore them. Say,

"I don't like to do that, Janie, and I know you don't like

[3] Ralph O. Blackwood, *Operant Control of Behavior*, Ohio, Exordium Press, 1971.

to miss that program. I'm going to help you to learn to come in when you're called so that you won't have to miss it again."

Give Janie a paper and pencil (assuming she's old enough to write) or have her respond orally to the four questions recommended by Blackwood:

1. "What did you do wrong, Janie?"
   "I didn't come in when I was called."
2. "What happened because you didn't come in?"
   "I won't be able to see all of my favorite TV program."
3. "What should you have done?"
   "I should have come in when I was called."
4. "What would happen if you had come in when you were called?"
   "I could watch all of my favorite TV program."

You may have to prompt your child, that is you may have to supply the answers. That's OK, because what you're after is to have her memorize that sequence. Go over it at least once more.

Next afternoon, say, "I want to make sure that you don't miss any TV tonight, Janie. Let's go over those questions right now before you go out."

Ignore any complaints as though you never heard them and go right ahead and ask the questions. Janie will probably come in promptly this afternoon when you call her. Just because she does, don't drop the mediation training. Repeat the process again the following day. Encourage Janie for having come in promptly the day before but insist on going through the questions again.

After a few days Janie's thinking chain will be automatic when you call her—something like this: "I'd really like to stay out longer, but if I do, I won't get to see my favorite TV show all the way through. I'll go in so I'll be able to watch all of it."

There are benefits from mediation training which go far beyond the specific incident in which it's used. For one thing, your child learns to look for alternatives to his behaviors and to weigh consequences. He also learns that long term rewards far outweigh the small satisfaction he might derive from yielding to impulse.

I want to add a word of caution in the use of verbal mediation. The system works only if what's at stake is something your child really wants. Janie, for example, really liked the TV show and was willing to modify her behavior so that she would not miss it. One thing that should never be used in trade, so to speak, in the verbal mediation training process is your love and affection.

Certainly it's desirable to reward your child's good behavior spontaneously with endearing words, hugs and kisses. But it is not only undesirable but dangerous to take away your love when your child behaves in an unacceptable manner or to give love when his behavior is acceptable. You should never say, unless you do thus and so, I will not love you. Love, if it's genuine, cannot just be turned on and off.

Psychologists point out that a girl whose parents "buy" her behavior with their love, may, when she becomes old enough to date, feel that she must buy the attention of boys with love. There is no research to prove it, but it is likely that prostitutes come from the ranks of those girls whose families exchanged love for favors.

Love should be expressed only when it is felt. If we wish children to grow up with that understanding, we cannot give love as a reward or deny love as a punishment. One right that children should have is the right to be loved by their parents no matter what their behavior.

We have covered a lot of territory in Chapter Two. You have seen how language develops. You should have a better understanding now of what you can expect at different ages in response to your attempts to change behavior through verbal commands. You should also have a few ideas of viable alternatives to your present means of effecting behavioral changes. In Chapter Three we'll talk a bit more about verbal mediation and you will learn some effective techniques from a method of behavior management known as "operant conditioning."

Chapter 3

Operant Conditioning isn't only for the birds.

ONE of my favorite stories concerns a mule. It seems that a farmer saw an ad in the newspaper which offered "a well-trained, docile and very obedient mule" for sale at a very reasonable price. The farmer was in the market for such an animal and so he jumped into his pickup truck immediately and drove to the address given.

When he reached the location, a farm about ten miles away, he was pleased to find the beast a very handsome one as mules go. He was also pleased at the way his new purchase obeyed his former owner and was surprised at how willingly and without hesitation the animal jumped up onto the truck.

When the farmer reached home, however, it was another story. The mule flatly refused to leave the truck. No amount of pleading, coaxing and cajoling could get him down. Finally the exasperated farmer put the tailgate back up, turned the truck around and headed back where he got the animal.

The man who had sold it to him was standing in the front yard of his house when farmer, truck and mule drove up.

"You tricked me!" the farmer accused.

"What do you mean?"

"I mean that this damned jackass won't do anything I tell him. Why, he won't even get off the truck!"

"Won't get off the . . ? Why, of course he will. Wait a minute." He turned and picked up a piece of lumber, hit the mule a resounding WHACK! on his rump and said,

"All right, mule, get down off that truck." The order was obeyed instantly.

"You see," he said, "you just have to get his attention first."

While I don't want to compare children and mules, although I've heard it done, there is a lesson in that story for us. What we're after in this book is a way to get children to listen. As with the mule, what we have to do first is get their attention. I think, however, that we can do that much better through the use of rewards than through the use of punishments, and that's the main thrust of this chapter. To find out how, let's turn back the clock.

The year was 1943. World War II was in full swing. As we have found out in the intervening years, the federal government, through its various agencies, was involved in many "top secret" operations. Specialists in many fields were recruited to work on these projects. Three of these were highly respected psychologists. The trio, B.F. Skinner, Keller Breland and Norman Guttman, were engaged in a research project in Minneapolis, Minnesota.

Hidden away on the top floor of a flour mill, the group spent many hours of idleness awaiting directions and decisions from Washington. Their minds, however, were far from idle.

In keeping with their scientific instincts, they became interested in the activities of the great numbers of pigeons which wheeled about the mill and landed on the window sills. The birds constituted an irresistible supply of research subjects. The three psychologists quickly became engrossed in serious experiments. But there was still time for frivolity. Skinner decided one day to teach one of the pigeons how to bowl.

The idea was to get the bird to propel a wooden ball along a miniature bowling alley toward a set of miniature pins. He was to do so by hitting the ball with a sharp, sidewise swipe of his beak.

The first obstacle was to get the pigeon to make the

desired sidewise movement, hardly a natural thing for it to do. To accomplish it, a situation was arranged which would "condition" the pigeon to perform as desired. Ball and bird were placed in a box in which there was a "food magazine" which was used to dispense food pellets.

The bird was observed closely. At the very first swipe at the ball, the lever on the food magazine would be depressed and he would be rewarded with a food pellet.

The scientists waited patiently. Nothing happened. The pigeon seemed to make every possible head movement but the one that was wanted. Time was not a factor, they had all the time in the world, but finally they grew tired of waiting.

They decided to try a new approach. Instead of waiting for a swipe at the ball, they would reward ("reinforce" was the word they actually used) any head movement which had even the slightest resemblance to a swipe. At first, even looking at the ball earned the pigeon a food pellet. Gradually the criterion was raised and performance had to be slightly closer to the final form in order to earn reinforcement. Each such successive approximation to the swipe delighted the psychologists and they were amazed at how rapidly improvement was shown. In only a few minutes, the ball was caroming off the walls of the box as if, as Skinner put it, "the pigeon had been a champion squash player."

What happened that day may have been fun, but it was also to usher in a vast new movement. The so-called "neo-behavioristic" psychology was to have an impact on virtually all walks of life.

In mid-September, 1974, a speech therapist with a school district was working with a little girl who had a severe language problem. The child, we'll call her Kathy, was a first grader. Her problem was that since coming to school at the beginning of September, she had not spoken. Not to anyone—teachers, classmates, aides or the principal.

The child's medical records did not indicate any reason for her non-speaking behavior. She apparently had all the physiological and neurological processes necessary. Beside that, her parents said that Kathy talked a blue streak at home. Apparently there was no payoff for talking at school, so Kathy didn't bother. She got what she wanted without having to talk.

When I learned about this case, I was reminded of the case of the boy who at almost fourteen years of age had never spoken a word. His family assumed he was mute until one day shortly after his fourteenth birthday he spoke for the first time.

He had just seated himself at the dinner table and raised the first spoonful of soup to his lips when he let go a barrage of blue language that went on for at least fifteen seconds. The only printable part of what he said was, "That's the hottest damned soup I've ever had! Burned the hell out of my mouth!"

His parents were as speechless as he was verbose.

"Why haven't you said anything in all these years? We thought you couldn't talk!"

"Well, up until now," he replied, "everything has been all right."

In operant conditioning terms, the boy's silence had been positively reinforced for all those years. All his needs had been attended to. Only when negative reinforcement was inadvertently introduced did he speak. But let's get back to Kathy's problem.

It happened that the speech therapist was trained in the techniques developed by Skinner, Breland and Guttman in the Minneapolis flour mill some thirty years previously. She decided to apply them to Kathy's refusal to talk.

Just as with the pigeon, the first step was to condition the youngster to talk. She would immediately reinforce the first indication of speech.

As Kathy entered the room for her first session, the therapist greeted her, but Kathy did not respond and, in fact, kept her head averted and would not look at her. Following the example of the trio of psychologists, the speech therapist decided to reinforce any response which had the slightest resemblance to the final desired one.

She made a clucking noise with her tongue. That got Kathy's attention and caused the little girl to look at the therapist for the first time. Immediately Kathy was reinforced with a smile, a comment and a protein tidbit. The child took the morsel and ate it, but looked away again. A few seconds later, she voluntarily turned and glanced briefly at the therapist. Again she was reinforced with a smile, a word of encouragement and another snack. By the end of the first session, without reinforcement, Kathy was looking at the therapist with regularity.

In subsequent sessions the youngster was reinforced at first for any sound she made; then, when making sounds in the company of the therapist was established as a behavior, a sound resembling a communication was required for reinforcement—a grunt of thanks, for example. Ultimately only whole words, and then sentences, earned a reward in the speech room. Finally, the therapist moved the treatment into the classroom so that she could condition Kathy to talk freely in that environment.

The approach used by Skinner and by the speech therapist is called "operant conditioning."

The theory behind operant conditioning is actually quite simple. It has to do with the fact that when a behavior results in a pleasurable consequence, it is likely to be repeated, and vice-versa. But the actual process by which desired behaviors are increased or established and undesirable ones reduced or eliminated is quite complex and follows precise rules.

Frequently, untrained individuals will read something on the subject and then attempt to put it into practice. The deceptive simplicity of operant conditioning often makes attempts unsuccessful, and the blame is then placed on the procedure; another case of the poor workman blaming his tools.

This chapter is not intended to supply the reader with the skills needed for the effective application of operant conditioning, but to give you an idea of what it's all about, so that you will have a better background for the use of verbal mediation. Here, briefly, are some of the major principles by which operant conditioning is governed:

1. Any behavior which is reinforced, which earns a payoff

every time it occurs, will be repeated. Loosely interpreted, a reinforcement is a reward. For example, if a mother hugs her three-year-old every time he picks up his toys, he will learn to pick them up. On the other hand, if she gives him attention—perhaps by scolding—only when he *fails* to pick up his toys, mother can count on having to pick them up herself.

2. It must be expected that the ultimately desired behavior will be achieved in small steps. The speech therapist at first was satisfied with the mere fact that Kathy looked at her. Then, as the behavior became established (repeated without reinforcement), the criterion of acceptable performance was raised. Each "successive approximation" of the desired performance was reinforced. That is, each time Kathy came even a tiny bit closer to talking, she was rewarded. This procedure was continued until the final form was obtained.

3. The choice of a payoff is critical. It must be something which the *child* considers desirable. For instance, I know of one case in which a teacher, unskilled in the use of operant conditioning, attempted to establish a desired behavior in a second grader by praising him in front of the class each time he exhibited the behavior. Instead of increasing the frequency of the behavior, the child all but stopped it. Had the teacher checked with him, she would have learned that his classmates were taunting him with being "teacher's pet" during recesses and after school. What she thought was a "positive reinforcer" turned out to be a "negative reinforcer." Positive reinforcers are those which tend to produce behaviors or cause them to occur more frequently. Negative reinforcers reduce or eliminate behaviors.

4. The behavior must be identified precisely. When behaviors are described in terms that are too general, they can't be dealt with. For example, when a parent tells me, "Betty is constantly trying to get her brother's goat," I have to ask, "But exactly what does she do, and how often does she do it? What seems to precipitate the behavior, and what do you or her brother do immediately after the behavior?" To put it another

way, behaviors can be dealt with if they are described in terms of what the child actually *does* that one can see and hear. Stating that a child wants attention is stating an assumption. Stating that she kicks her brother in the shins or that she throws temper tantrums is stating something observable.

5. In order to be effective, reinforcers must follow the behavior immediately. If a child misbehaves early in the day after dad has gone to work, a threat such as "Wait until your father gets home!" will not result in improved behavior. It only makes dad an ogre who will find it difficult to build a happy relationship with his child. Instead, the punishment (negative reinforcer) should be applied immediately and then the affair forgotten. Of course, if the child does something which is desirable, a positive reinforcer should be given immediately. This is true even though the desirable behavior comes right after a punishment. In fact it's especially true in that case.

6. Reinforcers should be as economical as possible. That is, if a smile and a word of praise and approval will do the trick, one shouldn't feel that it's necessary to rush out and spend ten dollars on a toy. In the first place, it's a delayed reinforcer and thus relatively ineffective, and in the second, it isn't required. Some children respond well to social reinforcers—praise, approval, etc.—others seem to need a material reinforcer *along with* the social. The words "along with" are underlined because the process includes switching from extrinsic material rewards to social ones and ultimately to the intrinsic reinforcement the child derives from knowing he is behaving in a manner which is in his own best interest and approved by significant adults in his life. We'll talk a bit more about reinforcers later in this chapter.

7. Behaviors which are not desirable may be reduced or eliminated either by ignoring them—giving them no reinforcement at all—or, as already mentioned, by using negative reinforcement. We mentioned temper tantrums, a common cause of the parental misery. There is only one way to extinguish that dreadful behavior. Ig-

nore it. Walk away. Leave the room. Leave the house, if necessary! According to the principles of operant conditioning, if a behavior is not reinforced, it will be discontinued. Negative reinforcement has been useful in the common parental complaint which I call "sibling quibbling." It usually turns out, on observation, that one of the children maneuvers the other(s) into fighting. What generally happens is that it is not the one who does the maneuvering who is punished, to the delight of the real culprit; it is the maneuvered. The treatment involves negative reinforcement (equal punishment) for *all* parties whenever the misdeed occurs.

8. Operant conditioning should be used to change a child's behavior only when such a change will be beneficial to the child. It should not be used merely to meet the need of his parents or teacher.

9. It can't be stressed enough that the child should be involved in the process, otherwise the whole thing becomes nothing more than a manipulation. For example, if little Hector has gotten into the habit of leaving all his toys strewn about the floor for mother to pick up, she should begin by making it clear to him that she doesn't approve of that behavior and that she intends to help him change it.

We've discussed verbal mediation which acknowledges the fact that the human is a thinking organism. The four-step thought process quickly and painlessly establishes the fact that undesired behavior produces undesired consequences, and desired behavior produces desirable consequences.

To give you an idea of how all this works in actual application, let me cite a case or two. First, let's take a fairly common problem, fighting.

Unfortunately, children have many examples which indicate that aggression is valued in our society. It pays off. As the saying goes, "Faint heart ne'er won fair lady." It's the aggressive person who is successful, earns more money and thus has more material goods than the unaggressive one. In other words, aggression is reinforced.

With this model for aggression, it's not surprising that your child will occasionally try to get his way by hitting others. But when the hitting behavior becomes excessive, it's a problem. Precisely how much hitting or how many fights constitute a problem depends on what you find an unacceptable level. Certainly a first grade child who gets into fights more than once a week should be dealt with.

Your first step is to get what's called a "baseline count" of your child's fighting. If he's a pre-school age child and you can observe him during the day, make an actual count of how many times he hits others. Count each day for, say, a week. Note what precedes the hitting. Does he say, "I'm going to hit you if you don't give me that toy," for example? Does he push or shove?

Also, as you make your count, observe what happens when he hits others. Often when the victim cries, his tears serve as reinforcement for the hitting behavior. Or the hitting may cause the other child to give up a toy he has been playing with; that too is reinforcing.

Your child will soon learn that if he wants to make others give up toys to him, all he needs to do is hit them. If he wants to make them cry, he hits them. The more he is reinforced for his hitting behavior, the more likely he is to continue hitting in order to get his way. Behaviors that are reinforced continue and become "stronger", that is, more frequent and more likely to occur.

How do you break this pattern of behavior? Begin by removing your child from the situation when you see the kinds of threatening, pushing or shoving behavior which you have observed precedes a fight. Isolate him for a short period of time. Tell him that he cannot play with other children until he decides not to fight, and that as soon as he has come to the decision that he wants to play without fighting, he can rejoin his friends. You must do this each and every time you observe the undesired behavior or its antecedents (pushing and shoving or threatening). This so called "time out" period shouldn't exceed five minutes.

It's important that the removal from the situation be done calmly, and in a non-threatening manner. After all, if you are aggressive and threatening in the manner in which you handle this, your child will learn that aggression is the way to solve his problems too.

The next step is most important. As soon as he returns to his play, be sure to observe what happens. At the first display of acceptable behavior, you must give reinforcement. Your child must learn that while hitting behavior has undesirable consequences, non-hitting behavior and cooperative play have desirable consequences. In other words, punishment without reward to compare it with is ineffective in changing behavior.

What kind of reinforcement should you give for playing without hitting? Children, as we said, respond very well to social reinforcers such as a hug, a kiss or a word of encouragement. Just your attention when your child behaves acceptably is a strong reinforcer.

If you're wondering why you went to the trouble of making that baseline count of the hitting behavior, let me explain. Parents too respond to reinforcement. As you continue your counting once you have begun to try the procedures outlined, you will probably see that the number of times fighting occurs has diminished. That's reinforcing of your behavior and it causes you to continue your program to reduce the hitting. Incidentally, don't try to *eliminate* the fighting. It's unlikely that you'll be able to do that. Try instead for a sharp reduction.

Let's recap that process. First you determine that there is a problem. Next you describe the problem in terms of what your child actually does. Don't say, for instance, "My son is aggressive." You can't count aggression. You *can* count the outward signs of aggression, though, so you say, "My son hits other children when he plays with them."

Next, count the number of times per day or per week it occurs, depending on the frequency of the hitting. During this period you handle it in your usual manner. At the same time as you make this baseline count, observe also what happens that seems to be reinforcing the hitting. It makes others cry, or makes them give up toys, etc.

Once you have the baseline count, change your method of dealing with it to the use of a combination of negative reinforcement, or time out, and positive reinforcement whenever desirable behavior occurs during play. Continue your count so that you can measure the effectiveness of your attempts.

It was mentioned that these principles are a gross over-simplification of a very complex process. I repeat that this chapter is not to be considered a complete guide to operant conditioning but as a background to the verbal mediation process. It is also expected that you will be able to use some of the techniques presented.

In addition to the principles discussed—and they are not all-inclusive—there are such added flourishes as "contingency contracts," "behavior graphing and charting," "token economies" and others with which the practitioner must become familiar.

If you're interested in pursuing this treatment, I have included sources of additional information in the bibliography. You might also talk with the psychologist at the school your child attends. Most likely he has had training in operant conditioning. If not, he can refer you to someone who can help you. Right now though, let's turn our attention to the matter of payoffs. I hope you will share the following words with your child's teacher. If he's not yet in school, then remember them when he is. It will pay off for you, too, in terms of a happier, more successful student.

A fellow school psychologist once remarked that the student population in our schools constitutes the greatest concentration of slave labor in the history of the world.

If you look at the definition of the word "slavery" in your dictionary, you will find something like "continued and wearisome labor or drudgery." For a lot of kids—far too many—my psychologist friend was painfully close to the truth.

Another implication of the concept of slavery is that there is no recompense for labors performed for one's master beyond the bare necessities required to sustain life. Certainly there is nothing to motivate an individual living in a state of slavery to improve the quality or the quantity of his services. This too parallels the educational experience too closely for comfort as far as a lot of children are concerned. Children need payoffs.

As adults, we perform the tasks required by our occupations for two kinds of pay. First of all, there is the salary or wage we receive. I think it's safe to assume that few, if any, of us would continue to report to our work stations for very long if we ceased to receive a paycheck. Pay, after all, is essential because it is one of what the behavioral psychologists call the "primary reinforcers," and it is the means, in our society, of obtaining other primary reinforcers such as food, shelter, clothing and so on.

But beyond the paycheck there are the "secondary reinforcers," those which are social in nature, like recognition, approval, promotion, praise, acceptance and love. And these too are essential, because without them we would not be motivated to bring any improvement to the work we do. I have known employers who managed to maintain a high standard of production and keep their employees in spite of the fact that their pay scales were substantially lower than those of their competitors because they knew the importance of giving recognition and praise when they couldn't afford pay increases.

The thing to remember is that there has to be a reinforcement, a payoff of some kind, or we adults will perform in an unsatisfactory manner ("goof off," appear lazy, or do our work in a sloppy fashion). Ultimately we will just quit (drop out). And there's the difference between us and that slave labor force sitting at their desks in classrooms all over the nation. We *can* quit; they can't.

It becomes pretty clear that for school children, denied the alternative of quitting by the laws governing public education, unless there is a payoff, all that is left are goofing off, being lazy and turning in sloppy work.

As has been noted, for adults payoffs are either primary or secondary. It's the same for your child. At home or school the primary reinforcers are things like grades and other direct indications that work has been done satisfactorily. The secondary reinforcers are attention, recognition, encouragement, promotion, approval, acceptance and love, just like those which serve as reinforcers or payoffs for their parents or teachers.

Consider for a moment what it would be like to work for an employer who graded your work every day the way we grade children every day on every aspect of their work. I'm sure that if I, like many children, got nothing but poor marks day after day, I would soon, as the British say, "pack it in," and either give up trying, or leave. At least I would have the comfort of knowing that I could go home at the end of the day and find love and acceptance and freedom from further criticism.

But for the kids it's double jeopardy! They get "zapped" by the teacher through the medium of failing grades (or those diabolical frowning faces that are stamped on the papers of primary graders who are still too young to appreciate the significance of an "F" grade), and then when they get home they are zapped again by their parents who, unhappily, feel that their child's failure is their failure. And then neither parents nor teachers can understand the reluctance of the youngster to do homework assignments, which are simply more of the same stuff that has been the source of so much psychological pain all day.

For the child who continually gets poor grades, grades lose their effectiveness as payoffs and so he doesn't try to get "A's", "B's", or "C's". Instead he has to rely on secondary reinforcers—social ones. But children are not very sophisticated or skillful socially, so how are they to get around the seeming impossibility of getting recognition from teacher when that social approval is reserved for those in the class who get good grades, not poor ones? Well, make no mistake about it, they will try and they will find a way!

At one extreme, there is the poor achiever who solves the problem by sitting like a lump all day. He doesn't do any work, but he doesn't make any waves, either. He is referred to as "poor little Billy, who is such a nice boy, but . . ."

At the other extreme is the acting out child. I said that children are not socially skilled, remember, so the aggressive child accepts whatever attention he can get, and even though his parents' attention may come in the form of disapproval, his little playmates may be undoing the hapless parents by giving him the approval he wants and needs. Don't forget that even *disapproval* from mom and dad means that they are giving the disapproved behavior attention and that constitutes a payoff for unacceptable behavior. You can count on the child repeating that behavior next time he wants attention unless his parents arrange for a payoff for acceptable behavior, such as giving him attention when he is playing cooperatively, as mentioned earlier.

It really isn't important that a child carry out a chore perfectly or even well, in fact. What counts is that his efforts be dealt with by his parents in such a way that he will want to continue trying. The payoff needn't be hypocritical. If the general appearance of a homework paper is terrible, don't tell your child it looks nice. Chances are that he knows it looks terrible, but it's the best that his fine motor coordination will permit at this time. Instead, find even one letter that he has done well and remark on that—or on the fact that the letters, poorly done as they may be, are all on or between the lines. Give your child some reason to continue trying.

"I like the way you made the "B"," will get much better results than,

"I can't read your paper. You'll have to try harder," or, at school, a frowning face stamped on the paper for all the world to see.

In time the child's neurological and muscular systems will mature and, unless he has been discouraged by then, he will gleefully be producing well done papers.

The point of all this is that children behave in specific ways only because they have been paid off for doing so. In order to have a happy, motivated and successful-feeling child, what you and teacher have to do is pay off work behaviors you want and ignore those you don't want. Here are a few suggestions:

1. Focus on the smallest *successfully* performed part of anything your child does and ignore the part, even

though it may constitute 99% of the work to be done, that was *not* successfully completed, assuming that the child tried.

2. When teacher sends home papers (and she will, because she believes parents expect her to), ignore the negative comments. Try to get her to make only positive comments on papers and report cards and to save negative ones, if she must make them, for a parent conference. Her goal should be, like yours, to make your child feel worthwhile. Finally,

3. Make sure that your child receives a payoff every day for something he has done well, no matter how small an accomplishment it may seem to you. The key is the positive approach. Reward, don't punish.

In Chapter Three you learned some terms such as "successful approximation," "negative and positive reinforcement," "conditioning," "social reinforcement" and "primary reinforcement." You have also been subjected to two very bad jokes, however appropriate. I apologize for those, but I won't promise not to do it again.

Let me leave you with the reminder that a little knowledge can be dangerous. Use the information contained in Chapter Three to back up your use of verbal mediation training. Don't go beyond that. If you do wish to try operant conditioning, seek out a specialist such as the school psychologist.

Because only the psychologically healthy child is truly able to listen, in Chapter Four we'll be talking about the kinds of things parents need to give their children in order for them to grow up psychologically healthy. There will be more about being positive toward your child, too.

Chapter 4

How to help your child develop the freedom to listen.

No matter where you live, I'll wager you have a Percy. Percy is the neighbor you go out of your way to avoid, but usually can't. My son called him "The Block Warden," because Percy seemed to know everything that went on in the neighborhood and considered himself some kind of local sheriff.

Percy was always borrowing things that he never returned, and that was only one of his annoying habits. In keeping with his sheriff status, he asked a lot of questions. A conversation with Percy was like being put on the witness stand. During my college days he would have earned a "What are you doing, writing a book?" These days, I believe, that translates to something like, "Bug off, man!"

Bothersome as Percy was, as the saying goes, it's an ill wind . . . I remember one day when I walked out of my garage to get the morning paper from under the car, and there he was, coming across the lawn. I thought of making believe the sun had blinded me so that I didn't see him, until I realized the sky was overcast. No use, I was trapped. I couldn't think of anything I owned that wasn't already in Percy's garage.

"Say," he said, advancing toward me, "I'm glad I caught you."

"He's more perceptive than I give him credit for," I thought, taking note of the verb he'd used.

"There's something I wanted to ask you," he pressed on.

"I'll bet," I thought.

"The wife and I were talking about you the other day . . ."

(The wife is Madge.)

"Mmm."

"And about what you do for a living . . ."

He made it sound as though I was the local drug pusher.

"I mean, you're in psychology . . ."

"Here it comes," I thought. "I'll bet he gets free legal advice from Bob down the street and free financial counseling from the banker on the next block."

"OK, Percy, what's on your mind?"

"Well, you know our son, Murgatroyd, has been having some problems in school . . ."

The school principal was a friend of mine, so I knew that Murgatroyd was in his office more often than he was in his classroom, and that the principal made more evening calls at Percy and Madge's home than an insurance salesman—none of them social calls.

"And you feel there may be something I can do to help," I finished for him.

"Hey," Percy gushed, "that's right! How'd you guess?"

"Oh, I'm very perceptive," I clucked. "It's part of the training, you know."

"Yeah," Percy agreed, "I know. Well, what do you say? Would you mind?"

"That depends. Just what is it that you'd like me to do? I certainly can't tell the school what to do, if that's what you . . ."

"Oh, no. We wouldn't want you to do that; wouldn't expect you to do anything like that. No, what we had in mind was—well, we're convinced that little Murgie's problems are the result of the way his teacher runs her classroom, and . . ."

"Of course they are," I reflected. "It has to be that

teacher's fault—that, or the hydrogen bomb fallout or sunspots."

"We have an appointment to talk to (not 'with,' notice) her and the principal about it."

"Mm hmm, and . . .?"

"Well, what should we tell them?"

"Good grief, Percy, I don't know! What did you have in mind when you asked for the conference?"

"How about if we just come right out and tell the teacher that we don't think she runs a tight ship, and that's why Murgie doesn't get along in school? If the principal won't do it, maybe we'll just have to."

"Well, I suppose you could do that, Percy, but are you sure that approach will get the results you'd like? It doesn't seem as though it would win you and Madge—or Murgatroyd either, for that matter—any points with the teacher, and it seems like you need her in your corner."

"You're right," Percy admitted readily, and I realized how neatly he had drawn me into the web. "OK, what do you suggest?"

If you recall my "it's an ill wind" statement, here's where it began to blow some good.

A plan began to form in my mind which would help Murgatroyd, Percy and Madge, the teacher, the principal, the school secretary who was probably fed up with taking care of Murgatroyd on his daily trips to the office—and the principal's wife, who rarely saw him in the evening any more.

"What I'd like to suggest is that you and Madge prepare a list of the kinds of things—the qualities that you think need to go into the kind of classroom environment that your son needs in order to get along. Take that list to the conference and objectively compare notes with the teacher. That way you won't be putting her on the defensive. You might find that she agrees with you on the qualities you have listed—or it may be a learning situation for all concerned."

"But I don't know anything about classroom environment—I'm sure the wife doesn't either. How can we make . . . ?"

"Maybe that's where I can help, Percy." My plan was beginning to work. "I do work closely with schools and teachers. If you'd like me to, I'll make up a list of the kinds of things you may already have in the back of your mind—the basic qualities in a child's environment that will go a long way toward helping him become a successful adult. But the school mustn't know I did it."

Percy grabbed for the idea like a quicksand-trapped man grabs for a rope, propelling my scheme further along.

"That would be great!" he said, turning toward his house. "And there's no rush, Doc, the appointment isn't 'til tomorrow afternoon at three-thirty."

"If we don't go on our planned Sunday outing," I mused, "I can get it done. Well, I didn't have to go into a helping profession . . ." I was just going in to try to explain all this to friend wife when Percy, golf bag slung over his shoulder, exited from his front door.

"Hey, thanks a lot, Doc, I really appreciate your help. See you later, I gotta be on the first tee in ten minutes."

I wondered how I could make my long-suffering spouse understand how I'd gotten into this latest imbroglio, since I really didn't understand it myself. I rationalized my entrapment, insisting to myself that it was in a good cause. I decided I would put off saying anything until I was asked what time we were going to be leaving for our favorite picnic spot, and sat down at my desk to prepare Percy's list. Thus began the final phase of my plan.

As I began writing, I completely ignored the school situation and began to enumerate the kinds of qualities I knew were missing from Murgatroyd's home life. The kinds of things children need in order to begin developing the freedom to listen.

After about two hours, I had whittled a much longer list down to what I would identify to Percy and Madge as five qualities for a successful classroom environment; one in which children could function without significant problems. When I was satisfied that I had succinctly and accurately described the blank spots in Murgatroyd's home environment, I telephoned the principal and shared the list with him, telling him of my plan and making him swear that he would not tell Percy and Madge I had done so. The principal was then to share the plan with the teacher.

When Murgatroyd's parents arrived at the school and began to tick off the entries on their list, they were astounded when they got nothing but absolute agreement from the principal and the teacher. In fact each entry was echoed so forcefully that Percy, who proved to have quite a bit of insight, began to internalize them—to realize that they had a relationship to himself as well as they might have to the teacher and her classroom management.

When I arrived home that evening, Percy was waiting for me in the living room, sipping my $13 a fifth scotch.

"I helped myself, Doc, you want one?"

"Yes, thanks, if it isn't too much troub . . ."

"You know what, Doc," he cut in, as he poured the drink, "that idea of yours really worked. I laid that list on the teacher item by item and there wasn't a single word of disagreement. That's one bright woman, that teacher. I was sure wrong about her. She said she could see the merit in each of the—what'd you call 'em—oh, yeah, qualities, and she said she was really glad that we had shared them with her and that she'd do her best to use them in her classroom the way we did at home. Yessir, a really sharp woman!"

"I'm glad you hit it off so well—should be helpful to Murgatroyd, I would think."

"I think so too, Doc," he affirmed, pouring another scotch for himself, "and there was something else about that conference. The more we talked about that list of yours, and how the teacher thought Murgie was so lucky to have a home that had so many fine qualities, the more we realized, Madge and me, that there were some things on it that we could use at home. Not that we don't already, you understand, but maybe we could do a little more, like the teacher said she was going to."

"It might help, Percy, few things are so good that they couldn't be better." Cliché number three, I thought.

"Well, I gotta go, Doc. Thanks. And thanks for the scotch, too. You can try mine this evening. You and the missus are invited over for dinner. Oh, by the way, Doc, could I borrow your electric drill? I broke the handle on your hacksaw and I can't use it until I fix it."

"Sure, Percy," I replied, as he headed toward the garage to get it.

" 'Bye, missus," he called over his shoulder, "see you 'round seven."

At this point you're probably wondering what was on the list I gave to Percy and Madge, so here it is. You may have a teacher you want to share it with or you might even want to compare it with your own practices.

The first thing I listed was UNCONDITIONAL ACCEPTANCE. I knew that both Percy and Madge were inclined to reject their son. For example, they made it clear that when he got into trouble at school, he was persona non grata at home, too. Your child needs to know that there is at least one place where he will always be accepted, no matter what kind of trouble he gets into; where he will always be loved and wanted, even though his deeds can't be tolerated. In order to accept himself, your child needs to be accepted by you especially, and also by those adults who are significant in his life. A child who feels accepted is willing to listen to his parents and follow their directives.

Next I listed THE FEELING OF BELONGING. Madge and Percy had a good marriage. They had always done things together and they continued to do so after Murgatroyd's advent, although he did, as they frankly admitted, cramp their style a bit. For that reason they decided to limit their family to one child. There's nothing wrong with that, of course, except that Percy and Madge were so close that there was no room for their son. He was never included in their activities and was almost treated like a boarder. If a child is shut out of his parents' lives, there's no chance for the kind of communicative give and take that develops listening ability.

The third item was THE SATISFACTION OF CONTRIBUTING. Madge and Percy are what I once heard described as "nasty clean." Madge is a meticulous housekeeper. Where most children might complain that they have too many chores, Murgatroyd was never allowed to help around the house. "He's so messy," his mother complained, "that I have to watch him every second. Even then I always have to clean up after him and do it over. It's just easier to do it myself."

It was the same with Percy. No matter how hard Murgatroyd tried, he just couldn't do anything to his father's satisfaction. "Sure he has chores, but I'd just as soon he didn't do anything—have to follow him with a garbage truck. I used to let him help, but I had to keep telling him to do it right, the way I do. It was no use. It usually got to the point where we'd have a big scene. He finally just refused to do anything at all."

No wonder the boy gave up. And the chores weren't the only bone of contention. Murgatroyd was a bright child. When he'd hear his parents discussing things, he'd try to enter in and give his opinion or tell what he had heard in school or on the radio or TV, but he was ignored. It wasn't surprising that he would do his best to disrupt classroom discussions. Percy and Madge took the teacher's suggestion that they have a short pre-dinner discussion time and include Murgatroyd. They told me afterward that they were amazed at how much sense the boy makes, and that he really understands a lot more than they had given him credit for.

The list had to include SECURITY. Children need to be sure that their parents will always be there; especially during infancy and early childhood. Murgatroyd never had that. His father frequently was gone on business trips that would last for a week or more. Usually Madge went along. The best he could count on was a baby sitter and he seldom had the same one more than twice. The result was that Murgatroyd was provided with every physical need, but he was emotionally hungry for his parents' love.

On his very first day of school, the boy demonstrated his insecurity by refusing to go. It was a real battle to get him to the point where he would stay at school once he got there.

Without feeling secure, your child can't develop a sense of INDEPENDENCE. Only when children know there is a firm, dependable home base to which they can retreat should their ventures into the world meet with rebuff, can they feel free to explore. Just as security breeds independence, the kind of insecurity Murgatroyd felt breeds lack of self-esteem and a dependent personality. The boy was afraid to try anything new and always needed his parents' or his teacher's step-by-step guidance to protect him from failure.

Maybe the two most difficult qualities on the list for Percy and Madge were the last two, because any change would have required a real sacrifice on their part. That's true for many of us. Change is a very hard thing to accept, whether that change is in others or in ourselves. But we must accept it because without change there won't be any growth. The way to begin to accept change is to accept one's self and what one is, here and now.

I must say that I know my list of five "nurturing qualities" is not all–inclusive. In fact, I'll add two more later in this chapter. But if you had a sufficiency of just those few when you were a child, you are probably a lot more open with others than most people and a lot better at listening to your child. And your child will learn to listen in part by observing the example you set in listening to him.

Most children today, I suspect, are allowed to be heard but few are truly listened to. Only their words get their parents' attention; their feelings are ignored. That's the real meaning of "Children should be seen and not heard."

If you are a parent who is shocked when you hear your little one utter a profane, vulgar or obscene word, let me tell you why you shouldn't be. First of all, your child is probably merely imitating an adult or another child when he emits that kind of language, so he doesn't understand what the word means. Secondly, in most cases he has heard the words used in anger, frustration, disgust or some allied feeling-loaded situation. That's what you should be listening to.

When a small child uses words that are generally expressions of feeling, it's likely that he has a strong feeling which his own store of words can't adequately describe. Restraints imposed on his actions prevent his expressing the feeling physically. For example, if he is angry at you he can't use physical force to express his anger by kicking or hitting. So he resorts to the use of a word he has heard an adult, maybe his father, use under similar circumstances.

Unfortunately, instead of ignoring the word and listening for the feeling behind it, parents most often listen to the word and ignore the feeling that prompted its use. The child is then punished for using a word rather than hitting or kicking, which are also punishable offenses. That's another one of those "double-binds" we spoke of earlier.

There's another unfortunate offshoot of this kind of treatment: When a child uses language and then is punished for reasons he doesn't understand, his self-concept suffers and his overall language development is hindered.

We must remember that small children use language in a very practical, pragmatic manner. Remember too, that small children are egocentric. They are not motivated to use language which is designed to be socially acceptable to their parents. Neither are they able, as we have seen, to express themselves in accordance with standard, adult grammatical rules. That produces other kinds of self-concept and language-related difficulties especially when they enter school.

Most of your child's first language output is concerned with his personal needs. He understands much more speech than he can produce and his verbal communication is often unintelligible. But in their pre-school years children have much opportunity to practice the use of language. One study showed that as early as four years of age, children may have a verbal output of twelve thousand words in a day. That doesn't mean twelve thousand *different* words, of course; it includes repetitions.

When your child enters school, you might assume that the new environment will help in increasing his practice in the use of speech. Unfortunately that isn't the case in the great majority of instances. On the contrary, the need for some kind of structure in which the concentration is on input rather than output of language precludes the freedom to speak. So following entry into school the development of vocabulary slows down.

By the time your child enters first grade, his listening vocabulary—the words he understands—is about 2500 words, according to most studies. Our researcher, however, placed the figure at an astounding 24,000 words! According to that same researcher, by the time your child reaches eighth grade, that figure has only doubled. Assuming that word count is accurate, and it's difficult to define precisely what's meant by "understanding" a word, one would expect a more rapid increase.

Aside from the inhibiting effect of the classroom situation itself, there is another reason language development slows down when children enter school: teachers tend to criticize children's incorrect grammatical usage. Parents, prompted by teachers' concern, also become critical of their child's grammar. The net result can be very damaging to the child's self-esteem relative to his ability to use language. To the degree that the child has lost confidence in his ability as a communicator he ceases to communicate and to listen freely, as he once did.

As your child grows, he develops what has been termed a "social self." It is through this development that he becomes socially integrated and compatible with the social group of which he is a member. As he experiences the attitudes and reactions of others toward him, he comes to have similar attitudes and to react toward himself in a similar manner. To the extent that he is encouraged by others, he values himself. To the extent that he is criticized and discouraged, he tends to demean himself.

If an individual comes to place a high value on his ability to use language, it is because his parents and other "significant" adults in his life showed interest in and respect for his use of language. It is from such backgrounds that the great orators and writers have come. Such nurturance also promotes the ability and the willingness to listen.

It's a difficult thing to try to select a group of factors which one considers critical or conducive to being an effective parent. I have already listed five. Let me add two

more. The first of these is the need to THINK POSI-
TIVELY.

As you would expect, I subscribe to a number of psychological journals and periodicals. A few days prior to
writing this chapter I received one which contained the
results of a survey of child-rearing practices in Canada.

The researcher concluded from the data he collected
that Canadian parents used techniques which were primarily punitive. Because Canadians tend to follow more
traditional "Old Country" beliefs with regard to parenting,
that didn't surprise me at all. The only reason I mention it
is that reading that report caused me to do some thinking
about the evolution of child-rearing practices in the
United States. That was certainly an appropriate activity
for an American psychologist at the beginning of our third
century.

Because of the religious roots of the founders of this nation and because of their own upbringing, they tended to
place rigorous restraints on the behavior of their children.
That continued until large numbers of parents misinterpret-
ed the intent of "permissive" educator John Dewey and
his supporters and later that of Benjamin Spock. A whole
generation, seemingly, was raised in circumstances which
were, at best, productive of will-o'-the-wisp disciplinary
procedures. The net result was confusion and insecurity.

When the offspring of that "lost" generation grew old
enough to procreate, they appeared to demonstrate the
same confusion and insecurity which characterized the
parenting they had received. Now their children are
parents and unless I'm mistaken, among this present post-
Spock generation, I see a movement back to the disciplinary and child-rearing practices of colonial times. I'm
not saying that it's a mass movement or anything of that
size; it's more like a rustling in a pile of leaves—but it's
there. However there's one vital difference. The negative
and punitive overtones which historically characterized
parenting have been discarded to a large degree. The accent on threat and punishment for wrongdoing is no longer the standard.

Right now I want to do a little name-dropping. At my

age I don't like to drop anything because it's becoming increasingly difficult to stoop over. But if you can recall the forties, fifties and sixties, you will remember Johnny Mercer. He was a famous songwriter of that period; a prolific producer of popular songs. But like many who have the spark of creativity, Mercer's productivity reached a nadir, a period during which the words and music just wouldn't come. Severe depression is typical at such times for creative individuals and Mercer was no exception. He turned to psychiatry for help. One day as he was leaving his psychiatrist's office, the therapist said something to him which was to become a turning point in Johnny Mercer's career.

As he drove home he remembered the words and they kept coming back: You have to accentuate the positive and eliminate the negative. Those words form the first lines of what was to become one of Mercer's biggest hit songs. They also became the basis for an entirely new attitude toward life for the songwriter. I'll explain what that has to do with my subject in a moment, but to put it in the right perspective, let me tell you about a young mother who came to see me recently.

It is my custom to ask parents who come to me for help, to write down as precisely as they can, just what the problem is. "My daughter who is in the second grade has begun to hit other children on the playground and in the classroom. Her teacher says that Susan is seeking attention and getting it in the wrong way," the mother had written. I had two immediate reactions to that.

To begin with, we know from our discussion of operant conditioning that the teacher had made an assumption that Susan's behavior was motivated by a need for or a desire for attention. We have learned that making inferences about the causes of children's behavior (or that of adults) is a chancy thing. But all right, let's accept that premise. The next thing that occurred to me was that the teacher had not only stated the problem, but had also solved it without realizing that she had done so; and that brings me back to Johnny Mercer.

The reason this teacher had missed the point, and the

reason most of us do miss the point when we come to grips with children's behavior, is that we're failing to accentuate the positive. Had the teacher taken the positive approach, she would have thought, "Susan is getting attention in the *wrong* way. What I must do to help Susan is to teach her the *right* way to get the attention."

I'm not singling out this particular teacher as a horrible example. Unfortunately, her negatively-based handling is typical of parents and teachers. I can give you an illustration of the truth of that statement from my experience in teaching classes on effective parenting.

When I work with parents, I generally start by providing each of them with an 8½×11 sheet of paper, which I direct them to fold in half and crease lengthwise. On the left half of the paper I ask them to list all the behaviors of their child (or one of their children) during the preceeding week which "drove them up the wall." Invariably, everyone in the class begins immediately to write down those misbehaviors and within a matter of seconds the left half of the sheet is filled. Next I ask the parents to list on the right side of the sheet each of that same child's behaviors during the preceeding week which were commendable. This time there's no furious writing, only head-scratching and brow-furrowing. It doesn't take long for the audience to realize that they've been had, and there are a few embarrassed chuckles as they get the point.

Why, I wonder, is it so difficult for us adults to accentuate the positive when it comes to the behavior of children? We can accept the idea that small fry need a lot of attention. When we don't give it to them they try, in a very unsophisticated fashion, to get it themselves—to force us to give it to them. This isn't premeditated behavior; as I stated earlier, children aren't socially skilled enough to engage in that. No, if they go about it in wrong ways, it's simply because we've ignored them when they went about it in the right ways. What we have taught them inadvertently, is that the wrong ways work, the right ways don't; and that's what they've learned. One thing I hope we're beginning to realize—behavior is learned, and we can teach positive behavior as easily as we can teach negative behavior. Now let's get back to the other point.

Try as hard as you can, because there are what scientists call "intervening variables," influences in the environment over which you may have no control, your positive efforts may still be met with negative behaviors. When that happens it sometimes becomes necessary to resort to punishment. Parents often experience much anguish and guilt feelings when they punish their children. They needn't, provided there is that overriding factor I hinted at earlier. If punishments have negative consequences for parents and children, most often it's because that factor is missing in that parent-child relationship. But I'm seeing more and more of it among young parents these days. What I'm talking about is that priceless commodity called love.

Not that they're the only ones who are loving, but take a close look at some of these youthful mothers and fathers. There may be some things about their lifestyles that upset traditionalists, but look beyond that. What you'll see in a lot of cases may be just as upsetting as their flaunting of tradition, because you'll see a disarming amount of love. Those young people aren't afraid to show their love for their children. A popular bumper sticker reads, "Have you hugged your kid today?" For some, this daring to care and to display that caring openly is a reflection of the love they received as children; for others, it's a reaction to parenting that was devoid of caring and love. No matter, it's there, and we can all take a page from their book.

The second point is—and I'm not advocating the use of punishment—when a child knows he's loved by his parents, when he receives an abundance of love, he can tolerate punishment should it become necessary, and there will be no need for guilt or anguish. If punishment is all he knows, that's another story. As with the first point, the approach is one that accentuates the positive first and foremost. Life with children would be so much happier and more fulfilling if we'd remember those two points and begin to act on them. So begin to look for the positive aspects of your child's behavior and reward these when you see them. As much as it's possible to ignore the negative behavior, do so, or you run the risk of rewarding it, never realizing you have done so.

If you feel a need to use physical punishment, if you have exhausted all other measures, be sure you have given your child reason to know he's loved, no matter what. Otherwise the punishment may cause resentment at best, and at worst, hate. And on that subject, it's interesting—and somewhat frightening—to know that when psychologists tried to construct a profile of the typical child abuser, there was only one commonality among those studied: all had themselves been subjected to physical abuse when they were children. That makes it critical to take great care when you resort to corporal punishment.

The last of the factors I consider essential to proper and effective child-rearing is ENCOURAGEMENT. Let's turn our attention to a discussion of this often missing ingredient.

On a recent trip to Europe, in a beautiful little square in Salzburg, Austria, I came upon an old building made all the more venerable by the large brass letters affixed to its second story. "MOZARTS GEBURTSHAUS," they announced, Mozart's birthplace.

As I stood looking at that building and the name of the composer whose greatness made it notable, I wondered about that greatness. What sort of family life nurtured the musical genius of Wolfgang Amadeus Mozart? I decided to find out.

Mozart's father, I learned, although a noted musician—he was concertmaster to the Archbishop of Salzburg—was not much for some other details. Had he been, his son would have been remembered as Wolfgang Theophilus rather than Wolfgang Amadeus. The composer was actually christened Johannes Chrysostomus Wolfgangus Theophilus. Instead of the Greek Theophilus, his father wrote Gottlieb, which in Latin is Amadeus.

Above all, the elder Mozart was a man who greatly loved his wife and children—so much so that he gave up his post of master of court music in order to devote himself to his family, and especially to the training of the young Wolfgang. He was also a father who knew how to get his son to listen—to him, and to himself.

In the Mozart Museum in Salzburg is a manuscript music book. At the front of the book are musical works written by various composers. At the end of one of these Mozart's father has written, "The preceding minuets were learned by my little Wolfgang in his fourth year;" later on: "This minuet and trio Wolfgang learned in half an hour, on the day before his fifth birthday." A few pages later is a short composition in completely professional, workmanlike form, alongside which is written, "By Wolfgang Mozart, 11th May, 1762." Mozart was just six years old.

I tried to imagine the kinds of conversations that took place between father and son. I could almost hear Mozart the elder saying, "You're really working hard on that minuet, Wolfgang. What is it about the piece that doesn't satisfy you?" or "I enjoyed listening to you play. How did you feel about your performance?"

About one thing I'm certain: The senior Mozart wouldn't have said "Good boy, Wolfgang, that was perfect!" No, I'm convinced that Mozart père understood the difference between praise of the art and encouragement of the artist.

The words written in little Wolfgang's first music book are a clue to the interaction between father and son. For one thing, they focused on the boy's accomplishments. They were not a reflection of his father's expectations.

When parents focus on their children's accomplishments, they're providing encouragement and helping them to develop positive self-concept. When the standard of behavior or performance is centered in parental expectations, the conversational sign is something like, "Good boy, Wolfgang, that was perfect!" That's praise. And praise can be destructive of self-concept. If a child has to be perfect in order to please his parents, he knows he has an impossible task. He expects to fail and he does. Soon he's failing at things outside the home, too.

There are some things you need to do in order to help your child develop belief in himself. For example, you should match your expectations with your child's abilities. Don't set your standards for your child too high. When standards are unreasonable, children get the message that whatever they do is not going to be good enough.

You need to realize that being the best possible parent doesn't mean that you need to have the best possible children. Parents who believe that are frightened of being parents because they fear their children won't be perfect. Have the courage to be imperfect and to have an imperfect child.

Your child comes to accept your expectations as his own. If your messages to your child, verbal or nonverbal, e.g., your body language, say, "I expect you to fail," your child translates that to "I expect to fail," and he will.

You should not make demands of your child which you're unwilling to make of yourself, or deny your child ordinary rights and privileges you insist on for yourself (excepting, of course, those which come with age, such as driving or consuming alcoholic beverages). If you do, your child feels that he's of less value in the family unit. If mother is the kind who leaves the breakfast dishes on the table until dinnertime, her children won't understand why they have to put away their toys the moment they're done with them.

If you expect your child to have a positive self-concept—to accept himself—begin by accepting him as he is, warts and all. Every child has a silver lining; look for it and encourage it. Your child won't improve in the ways that will give him and you satisfaction, unless he believes that he *can* improve. Would you feel worthwhile if you were constantly reminded of your faults?

Your messages, spoken or unspoken should say, "I know you can do it eventually and for now you should be satisfied with your efforts. Your mistakes mean that you're trying and you'll learn from them."

Be an encouraging parent, not a praising one. Praise takes away from your child the responsibility for his own behavior. It says, "If you do this I will be pleased. I will value you." A child subjected to praise comes to lose his identity. He is nothing but a reflection of the opinions others have about him. Ultimately he does nothing unless externally motivated. When that motivation isn't forthcoming and he refuses to conform, he is punished. He is made to feel unworthy. That produces behavior which is harmful because now the child must prove he is unworthy. Or fearing he will never again be able to earn praise, he doesn't try. Mozart might never have written another note following, "Good boy, Wolfgang, that was perfect!"

How do you know when you've praised? How do you know when you've encouraged? In general, praise is given in words that are judgmental of the child: For example, "Good boy, Wolfgang!"

In the first place, what is "good?" In the second place, whatever "good" is, does Wolfgang have to be good all the time in order to please? Or is he always good, no matter what he's doing?

Unlike praise, encouragement is directed toward helping your child develop the ability to evaluate his *own* performance—toward how your *child* feels about what he did. Mr. Mozart would more likely have said, "I enjoyed listening to you play that, Wolfgang. Do you agree that your technique has improved tremendously?"

Other statements that signal value judgments are being made, that child and behavior are mistakenly equated, and that it is praise rather than encouragement you're giving are: "You got an 'A'. We're proud of you." In order for that to be encouraging, it would have to be said even if the grade were an 'F'. Otherwise the message your child gets is that the only time you're proud of him is when he gets an 'A'.

Instead try, "After all your effort, you seem pleased with your grade," or "All your hard work really paid off!" The attention is given to how your *child* feels.

"You did a good job." By whose standard, yours, or your child's? In contrast, "What you did has been of help to all of us. We really appreciate it," is encouraging.

"We're proud of you." To your child that could mean he's OK with you because he's doing what you want him to or that his behavior is desirable because it makes *you* look good. An encouraging statement would go something like, "We appreciate what you did last week. It helped a lot to get that yard work done."

Praise judges the child and puts the praiser in a superior position. When parents praise, their children learn to compare themselves with others. They work only because "something's in it for them" and never learn to value intrinsic rewards.

Parents who encourage focus instead on their children's contributions to the family's well-being. Their children learn to evaluate their own behavior. They learn to be self-accepting, worthwhile, and willing to try even if it means risking failure.

In Chapter Four we have examined seven factors which, if included in your child-rearing, will produce the proper psychological climate for listening. We have learned that children cannot listen to their parents unless their nurturing has given them the freedom to do so. Children feel free when they have experienced *unconditional acceptance*, have a feeling that they *belong* to the family unit and are valued as *contributing* members of it. A child truly becomes free to listen only when he feels *secure* enough in his world so that he has the confidence *to act independently* of his parents.

We saw that *encouragement* and the power of *positive thinking* applied to child-rearing enhance the climate for listening.

Somewhere during his development your child will want to feel that he is independent. Just when that happens is different with each individual child. But when it happens, you will hope that he has been listening to you and that the standards—the values—that you have set will serve to guide him along the proper path. Whether they do depends on how clearly he sees his value system. So in Chapter Five we'll talk about how you can help your child develop clear values which he will "listen to" when he is faced with the many important decisions he'll have to make independently of you.

Chapter 5

How to help your child clarify values and make responsible decisions.

THE London Research Institute reported recently that most London boys engage in violence and one in ten apparently enjoys it.

In Sacramento, California, a six-year-old boy was beaten so severely at school by two other boys, aged eleven and twelve, that he required an operation to resection his intestine.

In Winston-Salem, North Carolina, two nine-year-olds and one child aged eleven extorted nearly $1,000 from schoolmates, starting out with threats of beatings unless the children turned over their lunch money, and graduating to greater demands.

In the 1971-72 school year, 23 percent of this nation's elementary school teachers reported student violence against them or damage by students to their property. In the same year public school vandals cost the taxpayers of Los Angeles $1.9 million and the bill in New York City was more than $2 million just to replace broken windows.

I'm sure we are all dismayed by the increase in destructive behavior and violence in our schools. What's even more appalling, we have seen the violence which began on the college campuses spread to the high schools and now to the elementary schools.

Recently I conferred with the principal of a primary

grade school about gang violence that was taking place there. Unbelievable as it may seem, the parent of one child actually "put out a contract" on a third grade boy! The father hired three other boys at a dollar each to beat up the third grader who, he claimed, had struck his daughter.

I'm not sure just what this country's ideology should be called at this point in time. We may still have Americanism, but from where I stand, looking backward half a century, that sterling label appears to have become somewhat tarnished. Looking forward an allotted score of years more, I hope it's true that the more things change the more they remain the same, because I can't help feeling that in many respects the way we were was much better than the way we seem to be becoming.

In spite of my misgivings, of course, I still prefer whatever "ism" we Americans will develop to any of the variety of "isms" I see abroad. But that should not rule out the adoption of anything which appears to have intrinsic goodness from other societies; even Communistic ones.

Back in our nation's childhood there was a strong sense of community. I believe that sense of community was still strong when I was a child—the two periods are much closer than I would like. People weren't afraid to "get involved" when others, friends or strangers, were in trouble.

I recall one day when a neighbor boy and I were coming home from school (we were seventh or eighth graders) and heard a girl's scream for help as we passed a heavily wooded vacant lot. Instantly we rushed across the street and, judging from appearances, prevented what must surely have been attempted rape. I wonder if that same incident were repeated today whether we would have chosen to get involved.

At least one family life specialist suggested that our children today suffer from a lack of watchful, caring adults within the community; adults who care enough to interfere—who show children that the way they grow is important to us all.

Psychologist Urie Bronfenbrenner of Cornell University traveled to Russia several years ago, and talking about his trip, he told how bystanders involved themselves in his disciplining of his own children. When Bronfenbrenner's son created a disturbance on a bus the boy was admonished by two or three women. When the psychologist's children got into an argument with some other children in a park, adults nearby quickly moved in and lectured the children sternly.

At first Dr. Bronfenbrenner resented the interference and was angered by it. But as he came to know more about the Russian people he learned that every Russian adult placed a high value on, and felt a strong responsibility for seeing to it that the nation's children grew up properly.

Certainly influences outside the home and school are important in shaping the attitudes and the behavior of youth. Nevertheless I believe there is a valuable lesson for parents and teachers in Urie Bronfenbrenner's experience.

I believe, for example, that much of the disruptive and destructive behavior of students would not occur if parents and school staffs became more involved; if they valued a sense of community. The home neighborhood and the school are, after all, microcosms of the world community, and the training ground for life in the community at large. Unless the inhabitants of the home and school communities have a sense of belonging, a commonality of purpose, the kinds of experiences which produce responsible citizenship are missing. Primarily this is a matter of providing models for the kinds of behaviors desired.

Many teachers do have a sense of school-as-community and do set the example for responsible citizenship, but many others do not. For example, I have often seen teachers ignore misbehaving children because, "They're not my students." On other occasions teachers have shown resentment if another teacher admonished a pupil of theirs. In the home community too, many times parents will ignore mischievous behavior so long as their child is not a party to it.

I have never been able to understand why adults go out of their way to discourage children who report their peers' misdeeds. The child who sees another breaking a rule and tells an adult is labeled "tattle tale." Is it any wonder that as adults these "tattle tales" choose not to get involved when they see a crime being committed? If teachers and parents ignore misbehaving children and criticize tattle tales, the result is confusion. The misdeeds and destruction persist and spread. Anarchism and tyranny can be learned at a very tender age.

It may not be easy to face, but adults must accept the fact that the destructive and frightening kinds of behavior in which more and more children are engaging is a result of failure to nurture them properly. A vital part of the nurturing is embodied in the provision of a home environment in which children are free to grow up. But it's equally important that every adult assume responsibility for seeing to it that children grow up properly.

From the day he is born, your child begins to become independent of you. How well he handles that growing independence rests to a great extent on how clearly you have permitted him to perceive and to follow a set of values which will be able to withstand the pressures of changing times. You can't dictate those values, you can only clarify them. As Gibran put it,

> "Your children are not your children. They are the sons and daughters of Life's longing for itself. They come through you, but not from you.
> And though they are with you, yet they belong not to you.
> You may give them your love, but not your thoughts.
> For they have their own thoughts. . .
> You may strive to be like them, but seek not to make them like you.
> For life goes not backward nor tarries with yesterday."*

As Gibran indicates in the last line of that quotation, parents must remember that they are preparing their children for life in the future, a future about which we can only conjecture.

It is hard to imagine a time when young people of all ages could be required to make a greater number of far-reaching decisions about their conduct. Behind whatever

---

* Khalil Gibran, *The Prophet*

decisions they ultimately make and forming the basis for them are the standards or values they hold.

Why does one youngster in a group who are throwing rocks at a school window refuse to do so? Why does one child work hard in school in spite of an uninspiring teacher while another, brighter one, given the finest classroom situation, does nothing? Why does one child decide to try drugs and another shun them? What causes one girl to try sex and become pregnant while still in school where another, in spite of many temptations, is still a virgin when she marries?

The alternatives available to youth today are seemingly endless in their variety. It's a bewildering time for them. The final choice is not an easy one to make. Because social standards are in constant transition, the world is filled with conflict and confusion.

It doesn't help matters that parents are also confused and bewildered. Helen and Sue Bottel, mother and daughter newspaper columnists, whose "Generation Rap" appears in some two hundred newspapers, discovered some of these inner conflicts. They surveyed about three thousand parents on a variety of subjects related to raising children. On the subject of sexuality, 45 percent of the mothers and 71 percent of the fathers indicated that they had premarital sex. Notwithstanding that, nearly 75 percent of those parents hoped their daughters would remain virgins until marriage. But only 40 percent believed that they would.

And although 50 percent of the parents hoped their sons would be virgins when they reached the altar, only 16 percent believed that would happen. The same parents then condemned this double standard.

There are indications that parents feel helpless in regard to the new moral standards: "The freedom to engage in premarital sex is here. Why fight a losing battle? Sex leads to drinking and drug parties . . . they're all tied up with rebellion and 'anything for kicks.' A parent can't win against the peer group."[1]

[1] As reported in the "Right Now" column, *McCall's* Magazine, December, 1973.

Similar conflicts were revealed with regard to other social mores. Drugs, differing lifestyles, dress and personal appearance also had parents on the ropes.

Parents do want to help. But their attempts fall short if they don't show their children how to be self-directing and to make their own correct choices. There are three major ways parents use in trying to help their children acquire values.

The first type of approach is in direct contradiction of Gibran. It is the one in which parents give their children their thoughts and transfer their values to them. This is probably the most frequently used method. One survey showed that 71 percent of parents believed that everyone should learn to accept the values of our society. Sixty percent believed that adults should impose their values on children. Again the confusion is shown in the fact that 91 percent believed that everyone should try to understand and tolerate varying lifestyles in our society.

The imposition of values might work if there were some kind of standard which was universal and unchanging. Unfortunately, as we are well aware, social values are in constant flux. Another problem with what might be called the "moralizing" approach is that each young person has to adapt to a number of sub-cultures. He may belong to a church, he has a peer group, an older child may belong to a political youth group, etc. Each of these may offer a different and conflicting value system. In addition, he encounters in one way or another individuals who also influence his attitudes and beliefs: teachers, political leaders, TV and motion picture personalities and so on.

With all this conflicting input, unless the child or youth has made a prior determination about whose advice to follow, he finds it difficult to make a choice. When he does make one, it is often an irresponsible one, based on inappropriate considerations.

What's missing in the decision-making of a youth whose value system was adopted perforce from parents who "preached" him into it, is a process. In order to make responsible choices, young people have to have some kind of systematic procedure for rejecting the undesirable facets of the many values which are being urged upon them and culling out the best.

Another conflict which arises when children yield to the moralizing of their parents in choosing a value system is the one that might be called "should-vs-do." Many times people who preach to others don't pay any attention at all to their own preaching. Parents may say, "You should do thus and so," and in their own daily lives do just the opposite. For example, they may preach about the evils of bigotry and racial discrimination and then join a movement to keep a family of blacks from buying a home in their neighborhood. All too often one witnesses the person who is a pillar of the church and exemplifies the golden rule on the Sabbath, but the very next morning is in the marketplace trying to cheat his fellow man.

A second way children assimilate values is through the medium known as "modeling." The idea is that if parents want their children to live by a particular set of standards, they will exemplify those standards. They will say, "You see what I do under these circumstances. I am worthy of being emulated and so you should do as I do if you wish to lead a life which is worthwhile."

It is indeed important for parents to provide examples of good conduct for their children. Unfortunately they can't expect that other adults with whom their children will eventually come in contact, will provide the same kinds of examples, based on the same values. A problem arises when those holding conflicting values and exhibiting behavior inconsistent with that of their parents, are greatly admired by the parents and/or children.

As an example, parents may provide a model—and the parables to go with it—of the strictest sexual mores. At the same time they express great admiration for a motion picture celebrity who is known to be following a sexual lifestyle in complete opposition to the one they would have their children follow. Or parents may profess honesty and in their daily living demonstrate that they would never accept a dishonest dollar. And then they will extoll the acumen and philosophy of a political office-holder who has been proven to be dishonest.

How does the young person who is exposed to such a dichotomy make a value choice when he is faced with one? If motion picture stars who are admired by one's parents can exploit traditional sexual standards, should one follow the example of his parents or that of the stars? If respected political figures can get away with crooked dealings, why not eschew mother and dad's preaching about the evils of stealing?

Let's suppose that the young person decides that he will reject in his own life any mores which run counter to those modeled by his parent. How then does he make room in his relationships with others for the differing life-styles they may follow? Must others who hold different values be rejected along with those values? Or is there some way of accommodating for them?

I have often heard parents say, "I do not make my child come to church with me. I will demonstrate that I go to church regularly and follow a particular religion. When he is old enough to make a decision, my child at that time can determine whether he wants to go to church and if so, which one he wants to attend."

The reasoning, perhaps is that there is no one religion which is "right" for everyone and that left alone, the child will eventually choose just the proper one for him.

A parallel to that would be for parents to say, we will not tell our daughter it's wrong for her to go to bed with any boy who might ask her. We will show her that promiscuous sexual behavior is not a part of our lives. Then when the time comes for her to have to accept or reject a bid for sexual favors, she will make the proper choice.

Unfortunately children usually don't make the proper choices if left entirely on their own. A laissez-faire approach to the transmission of values causes children added confusion. Parents have an obligation. They must not *direct* the course of their children's lives, but they certainly do need to provide guidance.

Forty-three percent of American parents, according to a recent study, follow the permissive or laissez-faire approach when it comes to giving their children values.

They think that whether to belong to a religious group and follow its principles, whether to "believe in the flag and in the Republic for which it stands," whether to marry rather than cohabit, and so on, are decisions that should be left up to the child. Those parents don't think any of those values are sufficiently important that they should see to it, to the extent they are able, that their children follow them.

In contrast, happily, the majority (fifty-seven percent) of the parents questioned do believe in religion, marriage as an institution, patriotism, the achievement of success, saving money, and hard work. These parents do want their children to have the same values and don't intend merely to leave it to the children to decide. How can they transmit these traditional values?

In order for a child to acquire values which are durable, that is, able to resist social changes which run counter to them, he must internalize the values. Moralizing and preaching won't do it. Simply modeling desired values won't do it. And certainly a laissez-faire approach which leaves decisions up to the child won't do it.

Children need the guidance of their parents in helping them think through conflicting issues. To be sure, there are parents who do try to assist their children in finding answers to the confusing situations they encounter. Few, however, use a systematic approach.

About a dozen years ago, with Merrill Harmon and Sidney Simon, Louis Raths, building on the writings of John Dewey, investigated the way people come to internalize certain standards and behavioral patterns. He was not concerned with *what* values you or I might have, but the *process* by which we came to have them; or how we clarify our values.

Raths identified seven sub-processes:

A. Prizing what one believes in and the way one behaves
   1. prizing and cherishing
   2. affirming one's beliefs and behaviors in social situations if it is appropriate to do so
B. Choosing one's beliefs and behaviors

3. choosing from alternatives
4. choosing on the basis of possible consequences
5. choosing freely
C. Acting on one's beliefs
6. acting
7. acting with consistency and pattern[2]

The approach used in "values clarification" is not one in which a particular set of values is instilled. It is one which shows the child how to apply the sub-processes outlined above to already held beliefs and behaviors and to beliefs and behaviors which are emerging and which will emerge.

Values clarification begins with awareness. Before your child can evaluate his beliefs and behaviors, he must be aware of what he believes and how he behaves.

Let's assume, for example, that through discussion and through exposure to your beliefs and behaviors, your child has come to believe it's wrong to steal. It is a behavior and a belief he will defend because he prizes and cherishes it. One afternoon when he is in a store with his friends, one of them steals a toy. The other children treat the thief like a hero. Your child affirms his belief by refusing to join in and instead urges that the toy be returned.

Because you have worked through with him the matter of stealing, your child chose not to take anything from the store, even though nobody seemed to be watching and it may have been easy to get away with it. He considers the consequences of such an action. If he is caught, he will embarrass his parents, he will be punished, the storekeeper will be cheated out of his profit and your child will be indicating that he believes it's OK to take what belongs to another. That would mean it's OK for someone to take what belongs to him. On the basis of those considerations, he freely decides to refrain from stealing.

On the next occasion when his friends suggest visiting the store, your son acts on his belief by refusing to join them. He has established, or at least is on the way toward

[2] Simon, Sidney B., et al, *Values Clarification: A Handbook of Practical Strategies for Teachers and Students*, Hart Publishing Company, Inc., New York, 1972.

establishing, a pattern of behavior which is consistent as far as stealing is concerned. The process begins quite early and there are some noteable milestones.

There's another word for this kind of governing force: conscience. Conscience is defined as "the faculty to decide as to the moral quality of one's thoughts or acts." It has also been called "an inner voice." True, it's an internal entity, but it develops as a result of outer forces. It's a system of acceptable standards and behaviors which is internalized.

In an excellent article on the subject, Dr. Allan S. Berger[3] points out that conscience begins to develop slowly during the first four years of your child's life, but it makes notable gains with the advent of language and the ability to communicate. By age seven, your child's conscience is fairly recognizable in his ability to control his behavior, and by the time he's ten, he behaves in stable and characteristic ways.

The small child begins to establish inner control over his behavior only because he learns that the consequences of doing what he wants are not pleasant. For example, as we noted, he earns father's and mother's disapproval. At the early stages, until he's about three, he refrains from misbehaviors only because one or the other of his parents is in view, or because he believes they'll catch him in the act, or discover his misdeed.

At around four, your child has to some extent internalized your standards. At least he knows that there are some things he should do and some he shouldn't do. He is not so much inclined to demand what he wants "right now," regardless of consequences. He is able to defer immediate wants in favor of longer range gratification because he is now able to understand why he can't get what he wants immediately. A major reason for this development is that he now has some sense of time and distance. But he is still behaving on the basis of rote, like the boy who said that he was four years old before he realized his name wasn't really "No, No, Bobby." He starts to do something which

[3] Berger, Allan S. "A still small voice that thunders," *Early Years Parent*, Vol. 1, No. 4, pp. 36-39, 1976.

he has been told not to do and stops himself as he thinks, "No, No, Bobby."

When he reaches five or six years of age, it's a different story. Now it is not rote, but a feeling of guilt that stops him from engaging in a disapproved behavior.

Children internalize parental standards through what's called "identification." A lad of six or seven comes to love antique cars because his father loves them, for example. Or a little girl of six unconsciously begins to emulate the mannerisms of her first grade teacher.

Through the identification process, children absorb their parents' values. They know what is acceptable to their mother and father and what is not, and behave accordingly.

Unfortunately, self-controls which are the product of identification alone, in the absence of clear values, are based on guilt and remorse. Breaches of the parents' code are to be avoided because they mean the loss of parental love and feelings of guilt.

Under such conditions, the child never becomes his own man in the moral sense. He is still very much his parents' man and when faced with a new, conflicting standard, cannot make a wise decision. Often the child who is governed by his internalized parent has difficulty in school because he cannot adjust to different standards which are imposed by authority figures there. Stories abound concerning the "preacher's kid syndrome." They refer to the fact that children who are raised under a harshly restrictive and inhibiting regimen, once free of their parents, often behave in ways which would be morally shocking to them.

When a child's behavior is totally what his conscience dictates it to be, he is never free to be himself. Even a *thought* of acting in a manner contrary to his conscience produces great waves of guilt. Because his conscience holds him constantly in check, he experiences a constant internal struggle between what he perceives as good (conscience) and what is evil (himself). He comes to believe that he is not worthy of his parents' love and so does not love himself.

Such conflicts can be averted if parents first help their children derive clear values and then accept the child's values. That doesn't mean they have to agree with those values, necessarily. When parents respect such differences and show that they trust their child to derive his own values, they enable him to respect and trust himself. When they help their child to understand that impulses which are in conflict with parental and social standards of behavior are normal, they help him to live in peace with them. When a child is not frightened by his temptations and impulses, he is able to resist them.

Now let's turn to the matter of decision-making, because that's what's at the base of helping your child to develop a value system that's viable and meaningful to him and acceptable to society. Decision-making and value delopment are mutually inclusive. One can't exist without the other.

As we have seen, values are defined as something one prizes or cherishes and which one consistently expresses in the way he behaves. When one faces a decision which involves a conflict of values, he must make an important decision. When such conflicts arise, there are often strong emotional overtones. It takes skill to arrive at a satisfactory decision, especially under such circumstances.

Rational decisions follow an identifiable course:

1. An individual is faced with two or more possible choices,
2. He examines his own beliefs and values,
3. He obtains as much information about the alternatives as is available,
4. In the light of the information gathered, he evaluates each of the alternatives,
5. He measures each of the alternatives against his own needs and values and selects the most appropriate, and
6. He adopts a plan which will effectively convert his choice into action.

Obviously you won't expect a small child to go through

such a process without help. He will need your guidance. Let's see how it might go.

Let's say that your child has been saving his allowance to buy a bicycle. He has about three fourths of the amount he needs. One day when he is with you at the store he sees a pocket calculator just like the one owned by the boy who sits next to him in school.

"Mom, I want one of those calculators. How about lending me the money until we get home? I'll pay you back out of my savings."

At this point *you* have a decision to make. You might say something like,

"No, I'm not going to lend you the money. I don't think you should buy it." (But that takes the decision away from your child.)

Or you might say,

"I don't have enough money with me. Let's talk about it when we get home. If you really want to buy one I'll bring you back tomorrow." (That still leaves the decision with your child.)

"Aw, gee, mom!"

"I'm sorry, that's the best I can do."

When you get home, you discuss the situation in this fashion.

"John, are you sure you want to spend your savings on a calculator?"

"Yeah, why not?"

"Well, let's look at the alternatives."

"What do you mean?"

"Well, let's see what your choices look like. For instance, look at it like this:

"You've been saving money for a bicycle. Do you still want a bicycle?"

"Sure!"

"OK, how soon do you want to get it?"

"As soon as I can. I can get Fred's paper route when I get my bike."

"What will happen if you spend part of your money on a calculator?"

"Well, let's see . . . One thing, it'll take longer to get enough money for the bike."

"OK. Now which is more important to you? Getting a calculator now or getting your bike sooner?"

"Well, I really want one of those calculators. Bobby's is really neat to play with. But Fred told me he's going to give up his paper route pretty soon, and I'd better be ready."

"In other words, if you buy the calculator, you might miss out on the paper route?"

"Yeah."

"Do you want the paper route?"

"I sure do! Fred really makes a lot of money and can win prizes, and. . . ."

"Is it important to you to be able to earn money?"

"It sure is. I could buy a portable radio and a stereo, and. . . ."

"And a calculator?"

"Hey, that's right! If I get the bike, I can earn enough money to buy the calculator."

"On the other hand, if you spend your money for the calculator now, you might not get the paper route. That would mean you wouldn't be able to buy the radio and the stereo. Or at least you'd have to save for a long time before you could get them."

"Yeah, that's right."

"All right, then, now you know what the alternatives are. Think it over and let me know what you decide."

You hope that John will decide for the bicycle and against the calculator, but if he doesn't, *you* must decide that you will go along with *his* decision. Even if his decision is not the one you think is best, at least you have shown him how to examine alternatives. And perhaps more importantly, you have shown that you trust him to make a decision and you have shown him how to examine his values.

In Chapter Five we have discussed values and behavior standards. Some information was provided about various stages in the development of values and the dynamics of the process by which this happens.

We have looked at the decision-making process also, and how this works reciprocally with value development. Finally, we "walked through" a hypothetical case so that you could see the decision-making process in action.

In Chapter Six we'll talk about discipline: what it is and what it isn't.

Chapter 6

How to manage your child's behavior—
without tears.

WE learned in Chapter One that the language we use when we talk with children often is confusing to them and doesn't make our intent clear. One can't reasonably expect a child to do what's desired if he's told in words that aren't understandable to him. But before you can put your wishes into language your child can understand, you must decide what you desire.

My experience is that parents nearly always have a set of identifiable standards. They know what they expect of their children. I don't think that I have any right to interfere with that set of standards. When parents ask, "Do you think I'm doing the right thing?", I refuse to answer directly. Instead I ask, "How are you going about what you're doing?" While I won't tell parents *what* to do, I will work with them so that whatever they decide, they can be effective in doing it. Of course there are times when there seems to be a need to explore alternatives to what's being done, but most often when attempts to get children to listen don't work, it's the language or the system that's at fault.

When I use the word "system," I'm talking about discipline. Frequently parents confuse the set of standards they wish their children to maintain with discipline. But standards are not discipline. Discipline is what your child must learn so that he will be able to maintain the standards you set, so that he will grow up to be the kind of child you desire, and so that he will choose to behave in a way that is socially acceptable.

As a noun, discipline is defined as "teaching or instruction." That implies a partnership. When used as a verb, discipline is generally defined as follows: to develop through instruction and practice or exercise; to train in self-control or in obedience to a given set of standards. That too implies a reciprocal relationship between the person who would "discipline" another and the recipient of the discipline.

But let me give you an idea of how parents often misunderstand and misapply disciplinary practices.

I was dictating reports one day when the telephone jarred my train of thought off the track. The caller was an apologetic teacher. "I hate to bother you," she began, "but I need your help." I assured her it was not a bother. "The parents of one of my kids are at their wit's end," she continued. "They've tried everything to discipline the boy—spanking, making him stay in his room, taking away TV privileges—Lord knows what else. Nothing works. He just defies them. I'm at a loss, too. Would you talk to them?"

Of course, I would. And we made the necessary arrangements. But, as I hung up the phone, I couldn't help saying aloud to no one, "Not another how-can-I-discipline case!"

To understand that reaction, you have to know that discipline comes up at least a dozen times a week in my work with parents, and that the same issue is always cropping up when parents and teachers talk. It wouldn't surprise me at all, in fact, to find out that the discipline question is one that hangs heavy over your household as you read this.

To be honest, even for the professional, dealing with discipline is tough. Part of the problem is that most parents aren't even asking the right question. It's not, "How can I discipline my child?" that you should ask but, rather, "How can I teach my child to discipline *himself*?"

What I'm getting at is that discipline is not something

you do to somebody. You don't turn it on a child like a garden hose to cool him off for a few moments on a hot day. That approach serves no lasting purpose and it puts the focus on the child, which is where it doesn't belong.

Where the focus should be, instead, is on the relationship between you and your child. If things are going well in the relationship, there's no need to try to impose discipline on the child, even if it were possible, which it isn't.

Maybe you'd never guess it from his behavior, but your child really does want to please you. When he doesn't, it's not necessarily because there's something wrong with him, nor because your "discipline" is a bust. More likely, it's a sign that there's a rough spot in the relationship. Smooth it out and watch the change for the better.

The approach to teaching self-discipline is from the front, not the rear. By that I mean it's a matter of leadership. If you set the example you'd like your child to emulate, he will. If the example you set is one you'd just as soon he didn't copy, it's likely that he'll copy it anyway. You can't get away with the "Do as I say, not as I do," approach.

Teaching discipline shouldn't be a power struggle. If, in your house, it's become that, perhaps you'd better examine your attitude toward your child. Learn to accept gracefully the fact that God gave your ever-loving the power of independent thought. Might as well, because there's no way in the world you can make him do something he's made up his mind not to do.

Not that a child won't change his mind—as we saw in previous chapters, he is likely to do so—if he's allowed to see for himself that the results of refusing your advice are unpleasant and unproductive.

I recall the case of a teenaged boy whose mother came to me for help with her son's lack of neatness. His room was a shambles, she said, and he never put his dirty clothes in the clothes hamper to be washed. She had to dig through the rubble on washday or he would never have clean clothes to wear.

"Is it important to him that he have clean clothes?" I inquired.

"Oh, good heavens, yes! He's a clothes horse. My washload is ninety percent his things."

"Have you told him to put his clothes in the hamper?"

"Of course, and pleaded with him, too. It just doesn't seem to get through to him. I've even told him if he didn't have his clothes in the hamper, I just wouldn't wash them."

"Why not do exactly that?"

"What do you mean?"

"I mean just don't wash his clothes if they aren't in the hamper."

"I couldn't do that. He'd go out of the house looking like a rag picker."

"Have your other approaches worked?"

"No."

"Then why not try it? Tell your son that next time his clothes are not in the hamper on washday, you will not wash them."

Did the approach work? You can bet it did.

Yes, you can change your child's behavior. And there are a variety of methods for doing so—each with its strong advocates and critics.

There is, for example, "operant conditioning," the brain-child of B.F. Skinner which we discussed in Chapter Three. Then there's the approach initiated in the 1920's by Alfred Adler, the famous Vienna psychiatrist. The so-called "Adlerian approach" was expanded in the United States by child psychiatrist Rudolph Dreikurs who produced the excellent book, *Children: The Challenge.** And there are probably as many other books, theories and systems on the subject as there are psychologists, psychiatrists and family counselors.

So what's a parent to do? Well, if you have all the time in the world, you might read everything written on the subject, and pick and choose those elements of each approach that suit your situation best. Without the luxury of that kind of time, however, it seems to me, you have two options: (1) You can choose just one of the professionally

---

* Hawthorne Books, Inc., New York City, 1964.

promoted approaches—almost all are effective, if properly applied—and follow it closely. Or (2), you can work out your own commonsense system—and then stick with it.

Home-made discipline is a lot like home-made bread. If the recipe is a good one, and the cook follows it with tender loving care, the result is indescribably satisfying.

Take the lady who came to me for counseling one day last year, ostensibly because she was concerned about her children's fighting (the children were 6, 10 and 12.) Actually, the fighting issue was a coverup for what was really bothering her: she was afraid she was too strict.

She strongly disapproved, for example, of her 12 year old daughter going "downtown" with her friends. "I know other mothers let their kids do it," she said, "but they let their kids do a lot of things I'd never allow mine to do."

Admittedly, if we'd had the time, I probably would have tried to instill in the mother the idea of teaching her children responsibility by showing trust in them. Since we didn't have the time, I decided on another way to help her: I told her she was doing the right thing.

An awful thing to do? Not at all. We have already talked about how, in this age of transition, parental values are under constant attack. Caught in the cross-fire of youngsters trying to shoot down traditional values and the psychologists and psychiatrists who are telling them what they're doing wrong, parents have been giving up almost without a fight. Is it really so bad to send in reinforcements to help the rare parent who is trying to stand his ground? Especially if the ground is solid?

The "too-strict mother" is a case in point. She had a well integrated value system and she knew what she wanted for her children. She respected them and she wanted them to be able to respect themselves. Why should I, or anyone else for that matter, interfere?

When I met with the children, I was sure I'd done the right thing. How did they rate their mom's rules: Too easy? Just about right? Too strict? Each of them, out of hearing of the others, said, "Just about right."

The moral for the reader and any fellow practitioners who happen to be eavesdropping, is that there are many parents who don't need to be "helped." Left alone, they do a fine job of child-rearing.

Still, there are some discipline principles—call them "Golden Rules" if you will—that most of us can agree on. I think of them as secrets everybody knows. No doubt you know them too. Some of these universal guidelines are presented on the following pages.

Experience has taught me that any method of behavior control that fails to make the child a partner in the transactions will fall short of success. Up to a point, the kind of behavior change or control that relies wholly on a reward system may work well. But somewhere along the line it has to be recognized that cognitive factors—the fact that man is a thinking being—can, and often will, defeat such a system.

Children are quick to perceive that they are being manipulated and they don't like it any better than we grownups. One fourth grader told me, "You're trying to use that behavior (modification) stuff on me. My dad told me about it. He tried it, but it didn't work." The message the youngster was giving me was that he was going to resist my efforts—successfully—just as he'd resisted his father's.

A junior high school boy told his school counselor the same thing, but with greater linguistic sophistication. "I know you're doing something to get me to stop cutting school, and I want to stop, but unless you let me in on it, I'll make sure it doesn't work."

The success of a democratic government hinges on an informed and consenting electorate. That's a truism. It is also true that the success of democratic parenting requires informed and consenting children to the extent that is possible. But like government, parenting must have a recognizable structure in order to make it work. In Chapter One we saw some examples of communications to children which missed the mark. Because the messages did not have a structure behind them, the children at whom they were aimed did not listen.

Here, then, is a structure. If you wish to use these techniques, they can help you develop in your child the kind of inner control that is necessary for self-disciplined adulthood. These suggestions must be used *in cooperation with* your child.

1. Describe precisely the behavior you want. Make sure your child knows exactly what you expect of him and then reward him for doing it. This is a much better approach than letting him try to guess what you want and then punishing him if he guesses incorrectly.

   For example, if your child is being noisy in the library, remember that "Behave yourself!" is not an exact and clear description of the behavior desired. "You must talk quietly in the library," is exact and clear. Rewards, by the way, don't have to be material things like candy, toys or money. Your child does want to please you. Letting him know he has done so can be a highly motivating reward.

2. Ignore slight misbehaviors. Don't reward misbehaviors that are only slightly annoying and unlikely to cause damage. Attention to them is rewarding. It's better to ignore these annoyances. When there is no reward for behaviors, they are discontinued. For example, I ordered a book from a literary club last year. The book never arrived and my letters got no results. Since my behaviors have not been rewarded, I decided not to order any more books from that club.

   If you have ever played a slot machine, you know that those "one armed bandits" are set so that there's a periodic payoff or reward. If there weren't, you'd soon quit putting your money in.

3. Don't "lose your cool." Control your temper when you deal with misbehaviors. Remain calm and speak quietly. It's perfectly all right—and advisable—to let your child know you're angry, however. Children learn to handle their emotions when they realize that strong feelings are normal, that you have them too, and that you can control yours.

   Can you imagine the confusion of the child whose mother told me that she was "curing" her son's habit of biting other children by biting him? "I show him how mad it makes me," she said, "by biting him anytime I catch him biting anyone. He's going to learn!"

What he'll learn is that if it's OK for mommy to show her anger by biting, it's OK for him, too.

4. Avoid arguments with your child. Once you have given an instruction or an order, or have given your decision (and you're sure you have been heard and understood), ignore any complaints and don't discuss it any further.

One of my clients disagreed on this point. She said that she made allowances at times when she felt that she might have been too strict. "After all," she insisted, "sometimes the kids aren't feeling well. They argue with me and make a good case, and at times like that I just don't make a issue of sticking to rules."

I pointed out to her that even when she's feeling her worst, she still has to obey that stop signal at the end of the street. As adults, her children will have many occasions when they will have to live within annoying restrictions. Parents who set elastic limits are leading their children down the garden path.

5. If your child is faced with an unpleasant task, let him know that you have planned something pleasant to follow it.

For instance, if there's a trip to the dentist in the offing or an especially long or difficult school assignment or a test he's really been dreading, being able to look forward to some favorite activity can help him—and you—through the unpleasantness.

6. Reward desired behaviors at once. For example, tasks should usually be completable in a short period of time. The length of time, of course, depends on the maturity of your child. The younger your child, the shorter the assignment, but reward should immediately follow satisfactory completion. Even though your child's performance may not be just what you desire at first, you will get where you want to go if you reward even distant approximations of the desired standard rather than admonishing below par perform-

ance. As performance improves you can raise your criterion for acceptable work. This is a very gradual process which, if done properly, has the added benefit of assuring your child of success every time.

7. If you must punish a misbehavior be sure immediately afterward to reward child's efforts to correct his behavior. Once you've punished for a broken rule, forget the affair. Don't continue to punish by withholding approval of the child's acceptable behaviors. The other day I noticed a sixth grader standing outside the door of his classroom. He told me that he was there because he had thrown a pencil across the room—the day before! He couldn't have demonstrated that he wanted to mend his ways and would not throw pencils ever again, even if he had wanted to.

.8 Avoid trying to get your child to confess to a misdeed. If you don't know he's guilty, he shouldn't be forced to confess. Even if you do know he's guilty, trying to force a confession will generally result in a lie. Tell him instead that you know he broke a rule and tell him exactly what he did. Inform him that you do not want him to do it again. Advise him of both the negative and unpleasant consequences which will follow his breaking the rule, and the positive and pleasant consequences of his observing it.

For example, stealing is a very traumatic thing for parents and very often children come out of stealing episodes convinced they are arch criminals. Stealing is a common behavior among small children simply because of the fact that it is wrong to steal is learned, not innate. When stealing occurs, tell your child that you know he took something that didn't belong to him and that you don't want him to do it again. Use verbal mediation training. Having made your point—and please don't try to exact a promise—drop it. If the behavior recurs, repeat the procedure.

9. Keep scoldings confidential. If you must reprimand your child, if at all possible, do it at the time of the offense, not the next day. But say what needs to be said quietly, and out of earshot of others. It's a terri-

ble thing to be humiliated in the presence of others, for children or adults, and it can produce hatred.

10. Teach responsibility. Train your child to be responsible for his behavior by offering him choices. This brings us back to the earlier statement that you can't make a child do anything he refuses to do. But remember that you *can* point out that there are natural consequences which will result from his freedom to choose, and then, if he insists on a course you advise against, don't interfere with the natural consequences. Of course you wouldn't permit a choice which would be physically harmful or dangerous. For example, the mother of a third grader told me her daughter refused to go to bed when reminded to do so. What should she do, she wanted to know. The child was cured of this behavior when her mother faced the fact that she couldn't force her daughter to go to bed. The child was free to choose not to go to bed, she was told, but she also had to bear the consequences, and the possible consequences were detailed for her. That night, when she decided to stay up late, fighting sleep just to make her point, her mother said nothing. It was not an easy thing for her to do. Next morning mother called her daughter at the usual time. Too tired, the girl immediately went back to sleep. When she finally did get up and get dressed and had her breakfast, it was obvious she was going to be late for school. "Will you drive me?" "No," mother replied. Since she had made her own choice about bedtime the night before, it was up to the child to bear the consequences. The approach was successful. It was much less fun to stay up late when it meant being late for school and having to make her own explanations, the child learned.

Sometimes, as we saw earlier, the natural consequences have to be given some help and artificial consequences must be arranged. An example of this is the child who refuses to eat at mealtime. Such a youngster might be given a time limit to finish the meal, at the expiration of which his plate is removed and he is directed either to leave the table and engage in some quiet activity or sit quietly at the table until everyone is finished. Another example is the youngster who fails to complete his assignments in school. He might be given a time limit for completion of the work, at the expiration of which his paper is taken from him and he is directed to sit quietly at his desk until the other children are finished. At the end of the school day he is required to remain until the uncompleted work is satisfactorily done. It's important that parents and teacher agree on procedures if such an approach is to be used.

11. Consistency may, as Shaw put it, be the hobgoblin of small minds. Nevertheless, if I were to rank in order a set of guidelines for sound disciplinary practice, I'd put consistency at the top of the list.

One afternoon I was watching Merv Griffin telecast from Las Vegas. One of his guests was a comedian who had a reputation for doing particularly zany things. Griffin's crew had photographed some of them. In one sequence, the talk show host was a gambler who happened to select the crap table at which the comedian was pretending to be the croupier. When Griffin got the dice, on his very first roll he got a seven. Elated, he expected to collect his winnings. Instead, the comedian/croupier scooped up his money.

"Wait a minute," said the unfortunate gambler, that was a seven!" He was to learn that the house makes the rules.

"Sorry, brown socks."

"What do you mean, brown socks?"

"You're wearing brown socks. If you roll a seven while you're wearing brown socks, you lose."

Like Merv Griffin in that film, I expect that each of us has been frustrated at some time in his life by rules which are inconsistent.

Do be consistent. If you decide that you want your child to follow a particular rule, make sure that the rule doesn't change from day to day. Make sure also that the punishment for breaking a particular rule is consistent.

Once you have established rules and they are clear to your child, you can stake anything that he will try to bend them. Testing for the plasticity of rules is something that seems to come naturally to children. Almost without exception, specialists in child behavior believe that parents should not budge an inch from established rules. To do so causes your child to be insecure.

One of the most insecure children I ever encountered told me. "My parents don't care what I do." It's a very frightening thing for a child to reach out psychologically toward the borders of his world and discover there aren't any.

On the other hand, one of the most secure children I have ever met was a fifth grade girl whose mother insisted that she attend school unless she was really ill. During her year in fifth grade the girl's father died. I was astonished to see the child in school the next morning. Her mother later told me,

"Dorothy knows how I feel about attending school. It's a rule we have. I believed that it was one stable thing in a world which was completely in turmoil, for her to attend school as usual. There was nothing for her to do at home."

Dorothy came through the trauma of her father's death much better, I think, than if her mother had relaxed her rule. I'm not sure that such extremes are necessary in adhering to rules, but it's better to go in that direction than in the other.

12. Avoid long lectures. Most children would rather have a spanking than a jawing. Beside that, you're just wasting your time. After the first few seconds, like the fighting boy whose father wanted him to "behave," your child will simply tune you out. I think the suggestion bears repeating; just tell your child what he did and tell him not to do it again.

13. Present a united front. If parents have a difference of opinion regarding discipline, they must settle it out of

their child's hearing. If there is a division, children will try to get one parent to side with them against the other—or vice-versa.

14. Keep your child separate from his behavior. This may be the most important of all admonitions. Your child won't listen to you if he believes that you think he is bad and unworthy. Regardless of his behavior, he should know you think he's OK. His behavior is unacceptable, but he is still loved. As long as your child thinks he's OK, he will believe he can change his behavior to conform to what you want from him.

In Chapter Six we talked about discipline, what it is and what it is not. You have seen that the key to effective discipline is communication, and that it is a cooperative activity. Some suggestions were given which can assist in teaching your child how to become a self-regulating, self-disciplined adult. As we have observed, in the final analysis it's a matter of how well your child listens to himself.

When parents inhibit their children from experiencing feeling and emotions, they are setting the stage for later problems. Children who are fearful of their feelings are unable to listen, either to their parents or themselves. In Chapter Seven we'll discuss how parents damage their children's ability to deal with feelings and emotions, and how they can avoid doing so.

Chapter 7

I'm so angry I can hardly talk!

STRONG feelings such as anger, hate, self-consciousness and inadequacy are cripplers. When you're under the control of strong emotions and feelings, it's difficult to speak—to state clearly what you wish to. Most of us have, at one time or another, uttered the words which are the title of this chapter. If not those precise words, then something close, such as, "What I wish I had said is. . . ."

Adults fancy that being emotionally "tongue-tied" is their prerogative and that only grown-ups have the problem. That's not true, of course. We must realize that children too become angry, feel strong aversion, have sensations of being inadequate and suffer from self-consciousness. We should be aware that under the influence of such strong emotional states, children like adults, are unable to express themselves verbally.

In this chapter we're going to deal with the problem that parents frequently encounter in communicating with their children: that of letting feelings get in the way of clear communication—speaking or listening. As a start, let's talk about awareness of self and awareness of the environment.

The first step in clearing the way for our communications with our children—or anyone else, for that matter—is to become aware of ourselves and our feelings. Only then can we become aware of the feelings behind other's messages. For many of us that's not easy, because at a very early age we were either tacitly or expressly taught to suppress our feelings. In our American culture particularly, even so noble an emotion as love is often subjected to suppression as children are growing up.

And so we become more and more inclined to talk about our feelings in roundabout ways as we move toward adulthood. Or we aren't able to identify feelings at all. We say, "I have this strange feeling—I don't know what it is," or, "I'm not sure just how I feel at this moment." In Chapter Eight we'll learn how this happens and how it can be prevented.

At the base of the difficulty we have with feelings is the pronoun "I." "I feel sad," "I feel happy." Who is this "I" we refer to? When you feel, where do you feel whatever sensation you are describing?

It has been observed that you have no direct contact with your environment. Whatever you know about it you judge on the basis of information fed to you through your senses.

If I say, "It's cold today," what I mean is that I am cold. I assume that what I feel is also felt by those to whom I say, "It's cold today."

My eyes tell me when it's day or night. My ears tell me when the wind is blowing if I am inside. If I'm outside, I know the wind is blowing because I can feel it on my skin, I can feel it resisting my movement as I walk, and I can see it blowing the branches of the trees. These are experiences which in the past I have associated with wind.

In our interactions with others, a particular statement arouses a particular feeling because it's played against information gained from previous experiences. For example, if someone makes a remark and I become angry, I am angry because my previous experience tells me that what was said was designed to hurt me in some way. If my prior experience tells me further that it is wrong to feel anger, I still feel angry, but I try to hide it and I now have another feeling: guilt.

Where is this anger exactly? Where does one feel guilt? If I have a previous experience which colors my reactions

to my environment, where, exactly, are these experiences?
Do all these things have a relation to me? Are they a part
of me, or are they, indeed, me?

The process through which we assimilate information
about the world is a very complex one. The auditory sense
and the visual sense are particularly complex. It's important that we remember that the ability to hear, to listen
and to use language are developmental. We discussed this
at length in Chapter Two. We know that there's more to
listening than meets the ear. One can be aware that someone is speaking but not hear, and one can hear and not
actually listen.

A few days ago I was seated in a restaurant. At the
next table the waitress was taking the orders of the pa-
trons. I overheard her say, "And what would you like,
ma'am?" The elderly woman to whom she was talking
said, 'I just told you! Weren't you listening?" The waitress
replied defensively, "Oh, yes, ma'am, I heard you, but I
wasn't paying attention."

In my work, I have occasion to do much driving in a
certain location of town. I must have driven on each of
the streets in the area at least a hundred times. I know
that I have looked at the street signs just as often. Yet,
were you to ask me precisely where a certain street is, I
would probably not be able to tell you. I saw the signs, all
right, but I just wasn't paying attention. I'm sure you have
had similar experiences.

As parents we wonder why we don't seem to be able to
get through to our children. We say, "Michael doesn't
seem to hear a thing I say." What we forget is that like
the waitress, children frequently hear what they're told,
but just don't pay attention. Each of us becomes aware
only when he chooses to become aware.

One objective of this chapter is to find out more about
the mysterious "I", where feelings are located, and how to
control them. We are going to become more aware of our
children's feelings. Thus in turn we can help our children
to increased self-awareness.

As we become more aware of ourselves, we also become
more efficient about processing and dealing with informa-

tion that comes through our senses. The need for efficiency becomes evident when we realize what an intricate pattern is involved in processing sensory information. Let's consider visual information, for example.

When you "see" something, you not only see it, you also perceive it, that is, you identify what you've seen. There's much more to visual perception than there is to vision. For example, if we both look at a cloud, we will agree that we *see* a cloud. But to me the cloud might resemble a huge polar bear. That's my perception. To you, however, perhaps it looks like a fluffy cotton ball.

When you read the words printed on this page, the actual process, immensely over-simplified, is this: first, what's called your "affective" state (feelings) is involved, since you "feel like" reading them. Next your "psychomotor" skills (your ability to use your large and small muscles) are involved because looking at the page means that you had to turn your body, head and/or eyes toward the page and your eyes had to effect certain delicate adjustments; finally, cognitive or thought mechanisms paired up words and visual images. Let's make a slightly more detailed analysis of the process.

First you turned your attention to the page. Next your eyes made the necessary accommodations and the images of the words were focused on the "receptor" nerves of the retinas of your eyes. Your optic nerves then carried the visual stimuli, not as words, but as tiny electrical impulses from the retinas to your brain; not just to any part of your brain, but to very specific areas and to very specific cells. What happens in the brain is believed to be a chemical process.

Thus far what is involved is what we know as vision. It's at this point—when those electrical impulses reach your brain—that the extremely complex process called visual perception begins.

Visual perception, then, is what occurs *after* the visual stimuli reach the brain. Where vision may loosely be likened to a mechanical process, visual perception is much more than that. It's the highly complex series of events

through which the brain interprets what the eyes have
seen.

Your perceptions are your interpretations based on your
past experiences—your frame of reference. For example,
take a look at that picture over there on the wall. We can
all agree that it's a picture. But when you looked, what
came into your mind first: the word "picture," or your interpretation of what the picture is about? Maybe neither
of those was your immediate impression. If you're the an-
alytical type, perhaps you "saw" a rectangular object composed of a frame surrounding a two-dimensional
representation of some sort of photographed or painted
figures.

On the other hand, let's assume that we're going to
identify all the rectangular objects in the room. We would
then include the picture because we began with the same
frame of reference. Now let's connect what we have so far
with the process of reading these pages.

If we all speak the same language and have an identical
code representing our spoken language graphically, we immediately have some things on which we can agree. We
all agree, for instance, that those written symbols we use
to represent the sounds of our speech are called letters
and words. We also agree, allowing for variations due to
ethnic background or sectional dialect, that particular letters and groupings of letters have particular sounds.

Let's assume that neither of us has a visual perception
problem. If we then look at the letters "d-o-g," we will
both have a mental association with a generally friendly,
four-legged, tail-wagging animal which is faithful to its
owner, likes to chew bones, whose natural enemies are the
mail carrier, the refuse collector, cats, and small boys who
pull its tail, and who has taught its owner to let it in or
out of the house when it barks.

What's supposed to happen when we look at the letters
"d-o-g," and normally does, is that the visual impulses
travel to the higher (on the evolutionary scale) centers of
the brain. There those impulses normally will be associated with "stored" information supplied by impulses which
came from the eyes, ears and other sense organs. From the

ears, for example, electrical impulses carry information along the auditory nerves to the higher centers of the brain where the areas of hearing are located. The information is then processed and stored in the auditory language cells. The visual image—the written symbol for the word "dog"—and the sound which the symbols represent are properly associated in the "language area" of the cerebral cortex, the most highly evolved part of the brain.

All this information is associated with previously stored memories, with the result that concrete and abstract concepts having to do with the word "dog" are formed in the cerebral cortex. Of course, if previous experiences with regard to "dog" are inaccurate, incorrect or in conflict, the processing system breaks down. The incoming information may be blocked.

The same problem exists when two people have a different frame of reference. To your child who brings home a stray dog, the animal is a source of companionship, something that gives love, and to which he can give love. To you it is a nuisance which you will probably end up caring for. You and your child thus process each other's messages against different perceptions. The result is that neither listens to the other.

Obviously, with such an involved process, even among adults there *can* be failures—and there often are, as you know. Among children, who differ from one another in their rates of maturation, there's even greater chance of failure. For example, the ability to perceive visual stimuli accurately may not be fully developed in many cases until the child is nine or ten years of age. Is it any wonder that you and your child often don't see "eye to eye?"

Considering the intricacies of perception and information-processing, it's easy to see how one could hear what his child is saying, but not really listen. Add to that the tendency to ignore the child's feelings and emotions, and the stage is set for parent-child conflict.

Earlier we noted that we know our environment second hand. We get information through our senses. Look at your shoe for a moment. It's a familiar sight. You know its shape and features. You know it's there because you are conscious of it encasing your foot. You know your shoe smells like leather and you know that you would be able to hear the sound if you stamped your foot.

You might find it hard to believe when I tell you that far from being solid, a shoe is really tiny bits of matter with space surrounding them on all sides, that as a shoe, its existence is tenuous and impermanent. You would protest that your shoe does exist. If I adopt the philosophical view that there is no such thing as your shoe, you might argue the point. But you would have a difficult time proving I am incorrect. For example, if you are not present in the same place with your shoe, can you prove it exists?

We assume that our awareness or consciousness of our environment is an exact picture of it. It is not, however. Your environment is what *you* perceive it to be. In the example I gave of visual perception, you recall that the image of the object one sees remains an image or picture of it only as far as the retina. Once it strikes the retina it becomes a series of electrical impulses and in that form is passed along to the optic nerve and on to the brain. Obviously electrical impulses are not an exact picture of the object that produced them. The recognition of the object takes place in the brain.

Do you think that you can see light only when your eyes are open? Try this experiment. Close your eyes and then press gently with your forefinger on the outer edge of your left eyeball, just at the bony rim. Go ahead. What did you see? If you followed the directions correctly, a small circle of light appeared at the right side of your eye when you pressed. Try the same thing with your right eye.

Even apart from such manufactured stimulation of the optic nerve, and completely apart from the eyes and optic nerves, you can still "see." In experiments at McGill University in Canada, and elsewhere, it has been shown that by stimulating the brain electronically, sensations similar to flashing lights are produced. That is, during surgical treatment of epileptic patients, electrodes carrying tiny currents of electricity are applied to the brain. When the current is applied to that part of the brain which has to do with vision, the patient reports seeing lights flash.

Such experiences are not confined to vision. Most of us, I would imagine, have had the experience of hearing a "ringing" in our ears although there was nothing in the environment to produce a ringing sound.

Lesser numbers of us have seen "a little man who wasn't there," or have begun sentences with, "I could have sworn I saw (or heard) . . ." And thank heaven that some of those creatures and experiences which are part of our sleep-state don't really exist, even though we "see" them in our dreams.

The picture we see through our visual system (eyes, optical nerves and brain) is not an exact one. In other words, it is not a mirror-image of the environment. The fact is that at a given moment, we probably process only enough visual information so that we can cope with our world. Much of the information is thus discarded. Only that which is necessary to help us avoid accidents, handle those objects necessary to work and play, and to survive, is transmitted to the brain.

When one is about to be run down by a speeding car, only that information is processed which is immediately necessary for survival. That there are other cars present, or other people, is not important and so is not processed.

A radio antenna brings in signals to a radio receiver indiscriminately. If there were not some system built into the radio to select among those signals, all you would hear would be a jumble of sounds.

We are "set" so that we handle incoming information selectively. We also have the ability to analyze tasks so that we can cope effectively with them.

The analogy of a road map is an appropriate one. It is not necessary that a road map be a faithful representation of every detail of the area. It is enough to know that a particular line on the map leads from where one is to where one wants to go. That the line leads across a meadow or up and down a series of hills, or that oak trees line the road are interesting but unimportant bits of information.

Moreover it is the process one goes through in using a road map that makes it a useful device. The map doesn't get the driver where he wants to go; it merely helps him get there.

It is the process one's brain goes through in using information from his senses that enables him to survive. Our ears don't hear, our eyes don't see and our skin doesn't feel. These organs merely *help* us to hear, see and feel.

Your environment, then, like beauty, is in the eye of the beholder. To repeat, your world is what you perceive it to be. Your experience does not exist in the environment, nor does it exist in yourself. It exists in the interaction between the two.

Jerome Bruner, a psychologist who did much research in the area of perception, showed that one's needs and motivations often determine what his experiences are. For instance, a woman might walk past the pet supply section of a market and not even be aware that there is one if she has no pet.

Furthermore, the completeness of our experiences determines our perceptions, as demonstrated in the tale of the blind men and the elephant. When asked to describe the animal, the first man, who had felt only its legs and feet said, "It's mighty and has great firmness, like a pillar."

The second man, who felt the elephant's ear, said, "It's coarse and wide, like a rug, a large thing." The third, who felt the trunk, said, "They are both wrong. It is straight and hollow, like a great pipe, an awful and destructive thing."

Because the experience of each of the blind men was incomplete, none had an accurate idea of what an elephant is like. Because each had experienced a different part of the animal, each had different emotions and feelings about it.

In Chapter Nine we'll talk about children and their feelings and emotions. But before we can deal with anyone else's feelings and emotions, we'll need to learn more about our own.

When you say, "I'm tired," you mean that you are attending to a bodily state or a set of bodily states you generally associate with tiredness. Your eyes may feel scratchy, your back may ache, your arms or legs may feel heavy and so on. It isn't awfully difficult to locate tiredness in your body if you push your consciousness of the feeling.

But what about, "I'm angry!" Where is anger located? When you're angry, in what part of your body is that anger centered? Many people would say, "That's easy! When I'm angry—really angry—I clench my fists. So as far as I'm concerned, anger is located in my fists." But does a mental event like anger really localize itself in one's hands or fists? A person's mind is indeed a part of his body, just as much as are his hands, but does the mind exist in one's hands?

We talk of feelings and emotions as though they were one and the same. When you have a headache, does it seem as though the pain exists separate from your mind, or is it a part of your mind? If you love someone, what is it you're feeling, and where do you feel it? If you're feeling "blue" and someone happens along whom you find entertaining, what happens to the blue feeling? Presumably whatever made you blue is still present in your life, so why and where is your "blueness" gone? The answer is that emotions and feelings are *not* the same thing, as we will see.

There are several theories regarding what takes place when we experience any kind of "unusual" state. By unusual, I mean any state other than complete absence of emotion and feeling, because emotions and feelings can range from very strong to very mild.

Psychologists agree that there are two identifiable reactions to emotions and feelings: when we experience them, we are either attracted or we are repulsed. Another way of putting this is that when faced by an emotion/feeling producing situation, we will react with fight or flight.

Imagine that you're driving along a two-lane road. Suddenly you become aware of an approaching car which has pulled out to pass slower-moving traffic. The car is speeding toward you in your lane. The driver has misjudged your speed and the distance between you. Seeking an escape, you look toward the shoulder to your right only to find it drops off so sharply that your car would roll if you moved in that direction. "I've had it!" you reflect in momentary panic.

I'll leave you to get out of that spot. I'm more interested in what kind of bodily changes you experienced at that moment.

We have noted that the senses convey information to "you" as tiny impulses of electric current. We said that these impulses probably cause chemical changes in the brain which result in that information being "stored." Now let's take the next step. In addition to being stored, incoming information which we associate with usual states has a more far-reaching effect.

Let's look again at that imaginary accident-looking-for-a-place-to-happen. Certainly as the driver of either car, you would not feel an attraction to the situation, nor would you likely be inclined to fight it through. What's uppermost in your mind after the initial helpless feeling is to flee the scene.

One widely supported theory suggests that in such a situation the following sequence of events occurs:

1. You immediately perceive that a car is approaching in your lane.
2. On the basis of your past experiences, you appraise the situation and realize that there is not enough distance between the two cars for the other driver to get back into his lane.
3. Your body reacts. In response to signals from your brain, the flow of adrenalin in the blood is increased. This causes your heartbeat to increase. More blood is pumped to your brain and other organs, increasing their efficiency. You next become aware that your hands are shaking and that you are perspiring.
4. You take action designed to save your life.

In that incident your emotions and feelings worked *for* you. Let's look at another imaginary situation: I hope you'll pardon me if I tell another story.

One evening a young man was returning home from a

date with his lady friend. The young woman lived on a farm quite a distance from town.

When he was about five miles from her home, he heard the ominous sound of a blowout. He stopped the car and inspected the damage. There was indeed a flat tire. No matter, he would put on the spare.

To his dismay, although there was a perfectly good tire in the trunk of the car, there was no jack to be seen. He spoke a few words in reference to the ancestory of anyone who would take a jack from a car and not replace it, and then peered down the road.

It was only eleven, but the road was deserted. Not a glimmer of a headlight was to be seen. Then he noticed that there was a light.

About three miles down the road, off to the left side, barely outlined in the light of the stars was a farmhouse, and there was a light in the window.

"It's a long walk," the young man said to himself, "but what choice do I have? I've got to borrow a jack!"

As he started the long trek, moving at a jog, he figured that it would take him about forty-five minutes to reach the house. As he jogged, he talked aloud to himself to break the absolute stillness.

"It's going on eleven thirty. That's pretty late for a farmer. He might go to bed before I get there." Puff, puff.

When he reached the two mile mark, as close as he could figure, he looked toward the farmhouse, just at the moment the solitary light blinked out.

"Shoot! Wouldn't you know he'd decide to go to bed before I get there. Anybody else would have stayed up! Doggone old man!" Puff, puff.

"Well, I'll just have to get him out of bed." Puff

"What if he decides to ignore my knocking. Can you imagine anyone doing that? Here I am, in the middle of nowhere and he won't get up to lend me his jack!" Puff.

"I'll just knock louder until he does get up. I'll show him. Ignore me, will he!"

"Y'know, he might refuse to lend me the jack, just to get even for my getting him out of bed. What a rotten thing to do!"

Just at that instant the young man reached the farmhouse. He ran to the front door and stood there, pounding on it with all his might.

In just a second there was a light upstairs and the window opened. The white hair of an elderly woman was highlighted by the bulb behind her as she leaned out the window.

"My heavens, young man, you gave me a start! Do you need help?"

"Not from you, you old toad! And tell your old man he can keep his damn jack!"

The moral of the story is that feelings and emotions can work against you. That's especially true if you let them run riot as did the hapless young man.

I'm not sure whether feelings produced emotions or vice versa in that story. In fact, the research is inconclusive in that regard. The important thing is that in the situation of the driver about to be hit by another car, fear played a part. In the story of the young man, anger was a decisive factor.

What concerns us here is the distinction between feelings and emotions which we mentioned earlier. We'll assume that when we speak of emotions, we're referring to body changes. Feelings are those psychological states which are associated with the emotions. We might say that feelings are the responses of "you" to current experiences as influenced by your past experiences. We'll talk more about this in Chapter Eight, as we deal with how your child's ideas of who and what he is influence his ability to feel and to handle his feelings.

With that background, let's get into an exercise which will help you become more in control of your feelings. You'll learn how you can make them work for you rather than against you in your role as parent.

Bernard Gunther, a psychologist whose particular interest is self-awareness asks, "What is life all about?" and responds, "Joy, mystery, experience, feeling, awareness, alive, love."[1]

[1] Bernard Gunther, *Sense Relaxation Below Your Mind*, New York, Pocket Books, 1973, preface.

Life is about all those things. In order to be alive, you must feel. Moreover, you must recognize your feelings as being part of you. You must be able to locate those feelings in your body. And since feelings are responses to body changes, you *ought* to be able to locate them in your body. You can learn to do this.

In Gunther's book there are many exercises designed to heighten awareness of feelings. Following is one which is commonly used as a starting point in courses which teach self-awareness.

Read the directions in the following two paragraphs carefully, and then do as they direct. The emphasis is on relaxation and really getting in touch with your feelings, so take your time.

I recommend that you find a comfortable spot on the floor and lie down. Close your eyes and lie still for a moment. Become aware of your thoughts. Let them into your consciousness for about a minute, then turn to your feelings. Concentrate on how you feel and what you feel. The thoughts will go away. For another minute or so, attend to your feelings. See if you can locate any tensions. If you can, how do they feel? Are you conscious of the pressure of the floor against your body? Where is it and how does it feel?

Next, relax each part of your body in turn. First your toes. Notice how it feels to relax them. Then your ankles, calves, knees, thighs, buttocks, stomach, back, chest, shoulders, arms, elbows, forearms, wrists, hands, each finger in turn, neck, facial muscles, eyes, forehead, nostrils, each in turn. Be aware of tensions that you didn't realize you had and how it feels to relax the tense part of your body. Become conscious of your own breathing and the sounds all around you. Become conscious of your*self* and how *you* feel at this moment. Then open your eyes. You should be completely relaxed.

You should repeat this exercise and practice others on a regular schedule. The idea, of course, is to be able to spot tensions and feelings quickly. Once you have acquired this ability, you will be conscious of it when interactions with your child produce interfering tensions. If you know they are there, you can control them.

When I say control, I don't mean that you try to push them out of consciousness. Far from it; you actually "own" them. You say to yourself, for example, "Little Arthur has made me feel anger. I am angry."

Then you are able to say, "Arthur, I am angry. When you don't come home on time I worry about you and I am angry that you caused me to worry." You may be surprised to find that Arthur will listen to that kind of message. It's much better than saying to yourself, "I'm so mad I can't talk!"

The result of owning your feeling in that way and then sharing it enables you to control it. But it also causes you to become conscious of struggles that go on within you because of conflicting feelings. For example, you acknowledge that you actually dislike Arthur because he doesn't seem to care whether his actions cause you worry. But one doesn't dislike one's own child!

That kind of struggle can have positive outcomes. For one thing, you begin to realize that you can love your child without loving everything he does. Do you really have the right to expect that your child is going to live up to your idea of what he should be at all times and in all respects? If you realize that you don't, it becomes much easier to describe your feelings to him when he runs afoul of household rules and regulations.

In Chapter Seven a number of points were dealt with, some lightly, some in greater depth. We have seen how parents often let their own feelings interfere with their communications with their children. We have stressed the thought that only by becoming aware of our own feelings can we deal with others' feelings.

We have tried to sort out the "you" who is a product of past experiences and present interactions with the environment and with other individuals. In some detail we talked about how information with regard to past experiences is processed and stored in your memory.

We saw that emotion and feeling are separate, although

inextricably interrelated entities. They can work for or against us.

Finally, we suggested an exercise in self-awareness. It was recommended that you follow through on these.

In Chapter Eight we'll examine in detail how your interactions with your child shape his ability to handle his feelings.

Chapter 8

As the twig is bent . . .

BEFORE we get into the main point of this chapter, I must digress for just a moment to discuss a related matter. When you want your child to listen, you expect that as a result he will either take some desired physical action or he will *restrain* himself from some undesired action.

In Chapter Seven when I talked about vision and visual perception, I mentioned that psychomotor skills are involved in those processes. In psychomotor skills too, children vary widely in their rates of development. Since psychomotor development is so basic to behavior, and since, as we noted, the end result of listening is generally physical action or self-control, let's spend a little time examining the subject.

Even though it includes the word "education," if you mention the term "psychomotor education" around a school faculty lounge, a school administrators' meeting or a parent-teacher assembly, you'll more than likely be greeted with a lot of blank stares. It isn't a well known concept, so it's not surprising that many school people, and nearly all parents, are unaware of the importance of psychomotor education and the need to incorporate it into the school's curriculum. But the fact is that such training could help to avert many school failures. It could also help to prevent many playground injuries and disciplinary problems.

For example, in one study involving some 10,000 children, which was conducted in the State of Maryland, it was found that the use of proper psychomotor training prevented 86% of first graders and 41% of second graders from reading failure. By the fourth and fifth grade, without such help, the percentage saved was reduced to about 15 percent.

In another study, two groups of children were given individual intelligence tests (the Wechsler). The first group was given psychomotor training once weekly for periods up to about sixteen weeks. The second group received no training. At the end of that time, this group's scores remained unchanged, but the group which had received training obtained I.Q. score increases as high as 21 points.

The relationship between ability to learn successfully and adequate psychomotor development has been well established in research. While it may be true that a lot of youngsters have been able to learn in spite of poor psychomotor development, there's ample proof that the lack of such development carries with it a high risk of reading and other kinds of academic failure as well as other related problems.

What do we mean by psychomotor development? To answer that, let's talk about the major aims of education—the so-called educational "objectives."

Education experts have arbitrarily drawn up sets of sub-areas of learning which are aimed at different "domains" of educational needs. Actually, of course, no such classification system can have completely separate areas, because children function as total organisms. All of us do. But for purposes of research, discussion and the planning of educational programs, the subdivision is useful.

One widely accepted classification system is composed of three domains. The first of these is the one that concerns the storage in the brain of factual information and data which are the building blocks of concepts. It's called the "cognitive" domain because it's most directly connected with the thinking process or cognition.

The second domain is what this book is all about. It has to do with the kinds of things that are most closely associated with the emotions of the learner; his attitudes toward himself and toward learning; his feelings. Unless the student is psychologically ready and willing to listen and to assimilate factual information, it won't happen. He also needs to have a positive self-concept and to be free of emotional inhibition to learning; as it is commonly phrased, he must have no emotional blocks. These things are involved in what's called the "affective domain," and comprise the student's preferences and dislikes, his interests and his values.

Schools appear to be doing a good job of cognitive education, perhaps in some cases so good that it almost amounts to force feeding. There are more facts than most children can digest. I recall the story of a fourth grader who asked his teacher a question about butterflies. He was directed to a book on the subject and was asked to do a book report on it. The report, when he turned it in the next day, consisted of one sentence, "This book tells more about butterflies than I really want to know."

Perhaps, had more emphasis been placed on the affective domain, that wouldn't have happened. In most schools, attention to affective education is far from adequate. But efforts are being made. For example, counseling programs are becoming available in elementary schools and more importantly, teachers are taking courses which deal with the area of feelings and emotions. Parents too are becoming more concerned about their children's emotional well-being.

But it's in the third domain, the psychomotor domain, that education (and home) are sadly lacking. Psychomotor education is concerned with the acquisition of the kinds of skills necessary to make full use of cognitive learning. For example, going through the physical motions of resolving an algebraic equation or an arithmetic problem on paper or on the chalkboard. Or using the hand and the eyes in coordination when copying work from a chalkboard. Visually scanning a page of print smoothly and accurately and using the muscles necessary for good, legible handwriting are other examples of psychomotor learning. But apart from the purely academic needs, in order to function properly at school—and at home—your child must be able to control his body.

As you can see, the three domains are so closely interrelated that, as we already stated, they are truly inseparable. Unless they are integrated in your child, your attempts to teach him self-control will at least to some extent be ineffective.

Consideration of psychomotor skills is particularly important if you have very small children. But even among twelve- and thirteen-year-olds there are gaps in psychomotor development. Many boys especially, tend to be awkward at that age.

I once designed a psychomotor training program for a school district which placed almost complete emphasis on the primary grades. But I soon found out that the assumption which led me to do so was incorrect. Intermediate and junior high school boys who learned of the special training also asked for help. One boy's comment was typical. "I don't like to go out for P.E. (physical education) because I fall over my own feet and the other guys laugh at me. Nobody wants me on their team."

I recall being told that the ancient Greeks increased awareness in their youth by having them stare at and memorize every possible detail on a coin. The boys were required to concentrate on the coin for hours at a time. I'm not sure that's a true account, but I do believe that if we taught children to become completely aware of their own bodies, we would do much toward increasing their ability to listen and to feel. We would also be helping them gain the ability to convert listening into desired action or restraint.

Some children move their bodies so inefficiently that to do so requires much of their energy and attention. For example, children who don't know the perimeters of their bodies—how much space they take up—tend to bump into things and to knock over cherished, and breakable, keepsakes. Children who don't have accurate images of their body parts tend to use those body parts inaccurately. For example, a child may fall over his own feet, or in reaching for a glass of milk, miscalculate the length of his arm and upset the glass—and mother.

We should not impose standards of behavior involving motor skills on children who are developmentally unready or who simply have never learned the skills. A child who is given a task for which his psychomotor skills are inadequate will not perform it successfully. He may even try to avoid doing it at all.

Parents who insist, "You could do it if you really tried," when their child brings home poor reading grades, may have a child who is developmentally unready to read. Similarly, the underachieving child whose parents tell him, "You're just lazy," may actually be avoiding failure. He doesn't do the work because he knows from experience that he'll fail.

It seems clear that the place to start working on listening skills is at the stage where your child begins to gain a sense of his own body-image. In the appendix of this book are exercises which will help your child learn where his body ends and the environment begins, and what his body can do. The suggestions are aimed at the kindergarten and primary grade child—ages about five to nine. If you have an older child who seems to be clumsy, I have listed sources of help for pre-teen and teenaged children.

We'll assume that you have a child who is aware of his own body and has a correct image of what it looks like. He knows his left foot from his right and, as Abraham Lincoln put it, knows that his legs must be long enough to reach from his hips to the ground. With that assumption, let's proceed to our analysis of how your child's ability to feel develops, how it becomes limited and how it can be expanded.

Psychologist Abraham Maslow[1] suggested that we are motivated to behave in certain ways because we have certain needs. The most basic of these are the kinds of physiological needs with which we are acquainted: hunger, thirst, sex, sleep, bodily integrity and relaxation.

The next level comprises those psychological needs

[1] Abraham Maslow, *Toward a Psychology of Being*, Princeton, New Jersey, Van Nostrand, 1962.

which come under the general heading, "Safety." We need a world which is orderly and predictable. To the extent that we see the world as just, consistent, reliable and safe, we are able to experience it fully. If our experiences lead us to think the world is unsafe, unreliable, lacking order and predictability, we tend to limit ourselves to those areas which are comparatively the most predictable and safe.

The highest level needs are those which Maslow termed "self-actualizing." When all the lower level needs have been met, we are free to exploit fully our potentials, capacities and talents.

The point is that if parents would deliberately set about the task of satisfying their children's needs, the children would have much greater perception of their environment. Children have needs for love, prestige, status and freedom. Unfortunately, in many cases parents attend only to the physical needs of their children.

We are careful to ensure that our children have physical examinations before they begin school. We see to it that they have a vision examination and a hearing examination. We know that a good, nutritious diet is necessary and we provide it. We are not so careful, however, about meeting their psychological needs. At school it isn't much better. In fact, often it's worse.

We hear the teacher say, "I just don't seem to be able to motivate Jennifer." What she generally means is that Jennifer isn't doing what teacher wants her to do. Actually, Jennifer may be spending her energy to meet some need of which her parents and teacher are not aware. If she is helped to meet her need, Jennifer might then be free to satisfy the needs of her teacher and parents.

It can't be re-stated too often that parents should consciously and systematically provide experiences which will indicate to their children that they are loved, that they are worthwhile and that they are respected. It is essential that children perceive themselves as capable.

A few years ago when the concept was new, I recall visiting a school in Modesto, California which was pioneering in individualized instruction. Each child's needs were assessed and an individual program was provided to meet those needs. A major part of the school's program was based on recognition of individual student achievement. The idea was to provide experiences which would virtually guarantee success at least a majority of the time and in a majority of efforts and then to reinforce the success by acknowledging it.

I was permitted to walk about and talk with students. I noticed one boy, about ten years of age who was lying on the carpeted floor, busily working an arithmetic problem.

"You seem to be enjoying your work."

"Yeah," he responded, without looking up or interrupting his activity.

"This is a new kind of school. Do you like it better than the old way?"

"Sure, man!" Now he looked up. His expression clearly showed that he thought I had asked a dumb question.

"What do you like about it?"

"Heck, man, before when teacher gave me arithmetic problems to do, they were too hard. I hated it 'cause I always bombed out. It's different now."

"How is it different?"

"It's simple, man, now *I can do it!*"

The principal later told me that this boy consistently had received failing grades. He had refused to listen to school authorities and so had been a discipline problem as well. Under the new program he was a different child. His improvement in arithmetic had spread to all his school work and he was no longer a problem. His parents, of course, were involved in the program too, as part of the school's strategy. They were amazed and gratified by the improvement in behavior at home as well as the improvement in school work.

The child who perceives himself as an "I can do it" person is free to be open. He is able to handle the wide variety of feelings his many life-experiences present. He says, in effect, I'm OK and if I have this feeling, since I'm OK, it must be OK to have this feeling.

I don't mean to imply that this approach should begin only when your child enters school. It must begin much earlier than that, although it's never too late. Even at birth your child was capable of a repertoire of feelings, although of course the number was limited.

The newborn infant is able to demonstrate only two feeling states: generalized relaxation or excitement. But the range quickly expands. At the end of his first year, the baby is capable of experiencing such feelings as anger, fear, disgust, elation, delight and distress. A three-year-old exhibits more subtle and more complex feelings such as affection for adults and other children, and jealousy, and these feelings become a permanent part of the child's memory.

In the research at McGill University which was mentioned in Chapter Seven, it was discovered that stimulation of the cerebral cortex at the memory "centers" caused the patient to recall past events. Not only were the events themselves brought into consciousness, but the feelings which were associated with them were also present.

The evidence is that feelings which were experienced in the past are locked together with the situations that produced them. When similar situations occur in the present, we not only *recall* the feeling we had in the past, but we actually *feel* the same way now.

Although experiences later on in life can alter personality, the most critical of these situations or events and their feeling components take place during the first years of life—up to the fifth or sixth year. They are perceptions which were imposed by parents, or perceptions of how one's parents behaved. These perceptions are assimilated by the child without questioning them. Together they form what we know as the self-concept.

Dr. Thomas Harris calls the many verbal and non-verbal messages which are recorded in the child's mind at this time, "tapes," or "tape recordings."[2] On the tapes are all the expressions of approval and disapproval, expressed and implied, of his parents.

Unlike the usual tape recording, once stored in the data

---

[2] Thomas A. Harris, M.D., *I'm OK, You're OK,*: A Practical Guide to Transactional Analysis, New York, Harper & Row, 1967.

bank of the child, these messages cannot be erased. They become a governing force which dictates how he will behave in the family and, later on, how he will behave in society.

To use Harris' analogy, another tape is being recorded at the same time as the one imposed by and perceived from the actions of the parents. To expressions of disapproval, for example, the child reacts by feeling negative toward himself. "If my parents don't think I'm OK, how can *I* think I'm OK?"

It seems normal to a child to relieve himself wherever he happens to be, without regard for the niceties of bathrooms and other social conventions. When he is rebuked for doing so, he is unable to understand the reason. More importantly, he gets the idea that there is something wrong with emptying his bladder on the command of nature.

If a child knocks a treasured knick-knack from a table and breaks it, he is greeted by a spoken reprimand and a facial expression which let him know unmistakably that he has done wrong. He feels, in a word, like a "klutz."

Parents who have unrealistic expectations of their children set the stage for conflicting feelings about himself on the child's part. For instance, I recall one child whose parents were told by a teacher that their son had a very high I.Q. The well-meaning teacher was reporting the result of a group test, the results of which are always suspect.

From that point on the parents told the boy that he was very smart; and yet, try as he would, the child could not get the kinds of grades his parents expected of their young genius.

Because of the frustrations which this produced, it was considered necessary later on to have the school psychologist do an evaluation. He found that the supposedly "very high I.Q." reported by the teacher was grossly inaccurate. The boy actually was in the range of scores considered average.

As psychotherapist Carl Rogers[3] puts it, when his concept of self is in conflict with his experiences, the child says, "I am very smart. I know I am because my parents tell me I am, and yet I have a completely different feeling. I get only average grades, even though I work hard. Even though my parents say I'm smart, I believe they think I'm dumb. I feel dumb."

Parents whose messages provide conflicting information run another risk in addition to the damage done to the children's self-concept. They lose the trust of their children, and a person doesn't listen to those he doesn't trust.

When a child has experienced a feeling which is inconsistent with his perception of what he is, it may take therapy later in life, if he has enough such contradictory experiences, to accept the fact that what he is is made up of *all* his experiences, contradictory or not. That isn't always easy or pleasant to face.

Whatever your child perceives himself to be is thus the result of his experiences. Who and what he believes he is comes from the verbal and nonverbal messages he receives from you and from other significant individuals.

Through this same process he gets his idea of what a person such as he perceives himself to be, should and should not do in particular situations. Moreover, ultimately he derives his belief with regard to what he is and is not capable of achieving, from your implied and expressed belief in his capabilities.

It may seem odd, but teachers are frequently astonished to see that when they give certain children encouragement and tell them they are "good," behavior deteriorates. The reason is that these children come from homes in which they are given the opposite perception. They feel that they are "bad," because their parents tell them they are bad more frequently than they tell them they are good.

The teacher's contradictory message doesn't compute, because it is inconsistent with the child's perception of what he is. His psychological survival thus depends on his proving that he's bad. It's not permissible to feel he is good.

Merely because he is led early in life to believe he is

---

3 Carl R. Rogers, *On Becoming a Person*, Boston, Houghton Mifflin, 1961.

bad or dumb doesn't mean that those self-concepts are unchangeable. What happens to him later on can have a profound effect in the opposite direction.

I know of one top-level school administrator, for example, who for years avoided higher education because he had been led to believe, from childhood, that he was not smart. Then, as a young adult, he was given an I.Q. test which belied his impression regarding his intellect.

It seems so simple to say, all right then, if you want your child to perform in a manner which is typical of the way a well-behaved child would perform, just keep telling him he's well-behaved. Obviously that's an oversimplification. You can't accept all behaviors. If you disapprove when your child relieves himself against the neighbor's fence, you can't very well reinforce that behavior with a pat on the head and a smile.

But neither should you react with a frown, a harsh word and a pat on the other end, much as you are tempted to do so. Depending on the circumstances, his age and his linguistic development, you should explain that this is not acceptable and/or you escort him to the proper location for attending to that bodily function. And it's essential that you do it matter-of-factly, without recrimination. That way he can still feel that he's OK. It's seldom easy to know exactly what to do.

Recently I was reading the Sunday newspaper and noticed an article that was so appropriate that I want to share it with you. It shows for one thing, that being a parent is not easy. Not the least of the problems is helping your child cope with his feelings.

The article was written by Richard Cohen, a reporter for the *Washington Post.** "How do you tell your son when to fight back?" Cohen asks. It seems that these days the answer is simply that one doesn't fight—ever, he says. Or at least hardly ever. Maybe if someone strikes you first, or to defend yourself. "But sometimes you don't do it even then. All those guns. All those knives. Save your macho. It can cost you your life."

---

* In the *Sacramento* (California) *Bee*, Sunday, November 6, 1977

At one time in his life, Cohen was convinced you should tell your child, "Never hit. Maybe not even when you're hit first." The violence of the Vietnam War and the assassinations were proof that violence breeds violence.

But Cohen wonders whether he has a right to tell his son to be the only kid on the block who never hits, who always turns the other cheek. There's a conflict between what the writer feels and what he was raised to believe.

But no matter about Cohen's conflict. His son was waiting for an answer. Cohen told him, "You do not hit unless you are hit first." He left it that way, but he hoped that the boy wouldn't come back later and ask, "What do I do when the pain of being teased is worse than the pain of being hit in the nose?"

His son left, confused, sensing his father's confusion about whether he should follow the dictates of his own latter—day values or go with the way he was raised. Cohen, watching his son walk away, wondered, in effect, whether part of the puberty rite in Western civilization is the requirement that a child take measure of his own courage.

As we all do when, as parents, we aren't sure of the proper course, Cohen fell back on what had worked for him when he was growing up. The thing is, he did tell his son what to do. He made the decision; and it was one that neither was comfortable with.

I wonder how you would handle that question at this point. Would you say, "It's all right to hit provided . . ." or would you involve your child and his feelings in the decision-making process? If you're not sure, you might want to go back and read Chapter Five again. In any case, Cohen's experience shows how difficult it is to help your child deal with his feelings when your own get in the way. In part, at least, it's a matter of deciding whether you want to permit your child to express his feelings or whether you want to control his feelings and his expression of them.

A number of studies have been done of differences in home environments and their effects on the development of personality and emotional adjustment. Two classifications were used to characterize the differences: "democratic" and "controlled."

Democratic homes are those in which there is a greater degree of permissiveness, much verbal give and take between parents and child and involvement of the child in decisions. In such homes were found the qualities of outgoingness, assertiveness, activity, leadership and warmth. They provided strong emotional support for the child.

Children from democratic homes were more original in their thinking, more creative, constructive and curious than those from other homes. But they were also more disobedient and nonconforming. They were relatively uninhibited in expressing feelings.

Other studies of children between ages four and six have shown that democratic homes produce children who are less argumentative, more responsive to praise and blame, more considerate, more successful socially than those from controlled homes and more able to deal with their feelings.

Where the home environment is controlled, that is where there is an excessive number of rules, many "thou shalts" and "thou shalt nots," children tend to be quiet, shy, inhibited, conforming, socially unassertive and lacking in creativity and curiosity. If overattention and indulgence are added, children show such behaviors as dawdling, dependence, and lack of persistence. They also cry easily, tend to be withdrawn, have poor psychomotor development, and are afraid of physical activity.

Psychologist Paul H. Mussen interprets the findings of those studies in terms of what's called "social learning theory." He points out that "Permissive, democratic homes encourage and reward curiosity, exploration . . . and the expression of ideas and feelings . . . The child who is controlled or overprotected by his parents does not learn these kinds of responses, because he is discouraged from acting independently . . . He acquires timid, awkward, apprehensive, and generally conforming responses."[4]

There's an important consideration in encouraging inde-

[4] Paul H. Mussen, *The Psychological Development of the Child*, New York, Prentice-Hall, 1963, p. 72.

pendence and assertiveness in your child. These are certainly desirable qualities, but they can also cause some problems. Children from democratic homes, for example, tend to be uninhibited, independent and assertive with regard to authority figures. Since they are raised in an atmosphere which encourages participation in decision-making, they have difficulty accepting rules without question. If they feel dislike for anyone, they express that feeling to the object of their dislike. It doesn't matter if the person happens to be a teacher or other authority figure.

So you have a decision to make. Do you want your child to become a feeling, independent, creative, socially successful adult? You may have a price to pay. For example, there may be frequent trips to school to talk with teacher and/or principal. But on your side is the fact that your child will be both willing and able to search for solutions to the problems his nonconformity causes. He probably won't compromise his beliefs and feelings, but he will be able to accommodate them and live in harmony with his environment and with those who share it.

Chapter Eight was about feelings. Specifically, your child's feelings. The intent was to show you how your interactions with him determine not only his ability to *handle* his feelings, but also *how* he feels about himself.

Because your approval is so important, your child wants to do as you would like. But he is not a forty-year-old midget. He does not have the motor skills necessary to accomplish all the tasks you might expect of him. Often it is his inability to control his body that brings your disapproval. I have suggested some ways you can enhance motor development.

We have seen that children have basic needs which go far beyond the purely physical ones. In effect, when you demand certain kinds of performance, you are indicating *your* needs, and *your* desire that your child meet those needs. But he cannot be expected to do so unless *his* needs are met. He is still at a lower needs level. He wants to experience your approval, but he is not free to seek it, or he would.

For example, in order to feel positively about himself,

your child must believe that he is a "can-do" person. You can meet his need to have that kind of positive feeling by letting him know that *you* think he's a can-do person. That can help open the door for him and allow him to let in as many feelings as his life experiences present.

But don't tell your child you believe in him if you don't really mean it. Don't let your feelings and your belief become incongruent. Your child will know it if you do and he will become confused. Worse, he won't trust you in the future, he won't listen to what you ask of him, and he won't trust his own feelings.

In Chapter Nine we're going to examine the differences between thoughts and feelings. You'll see how you can use one to clarify the other so that you can communicate more effectively with your child.

Chapter 9

It is *not* all in your mind!

It's a fairly safe bet that some well-meaning soul has responded to your concern about a situation with the words, "Don't worry about it, it's all in your mind." Of course you know very well that it *isn't* all in your mind. If, for example, a good friend has done something which damages you in some way, you don't simply think, "Oh dear! Sally betrayed my trust in her." Not by a long shot. You experience it deep "inside."

A situation such as that involves three facets of your being: thought, feeling, and emotion, and you need to know more about how each operates. Let's discuss the distinction between feeling and emotion first, then we'll deal with the difference between thinking and feeling. Finally, we'll examine the difference between expressing your feelings and describing them.

To begin our discussion, let me repeat a statement made in Chapter Seven, regarding the difference between feeling and motion: Feelings are mental events, emotions are the physical or body changes which accompany feelings. Now having made that simple statement, let's examine what it means.

Today it is thought that emotional response is not specific, but generalized. That is, no matter what the situation one experiences, the emotion is the same. Let me explain that in more detail.

Even in slightly threatening circumstances, there are slight changes in your body state. Whether the emotion is a response to a feeling of love, hate, danger, anger, excitement or adventure, your physiological responses are the same.

If you are faced with a problem, even one of moderate difficulty, almost every part of your body accelerates its activity to help you cope with it. You are ready to solve it.

Emotion is a speeding up of bodily processes which is most clearly experienced when there is a strong demand for action. As we have observed in Chapter Seven, one perspires, he is conscious of a surge of energy due to the release of blood sugar, his rate of breathing and his pulse rate accelerate, and, should there be danger of physical injury, his blood is prepared to coagulate more quickly because of the increased activity of his adrenal glands. These responses are the same, as we have noted, no matter what the emotion. Only the degree of activity varies with the strength of the emotion.

The entire process has been likened to mobilizing a nation's resources for impending war. Placing the human organism on a "war footing" by mobilizing all physiological resources enables one to meet, or to flee from the source of, danger or threat.

That's a bit different concept from the usual one which holds that we are under the control of our emotions. Indeed, what is proposed is that emotions can aid us in coping with a threatening situation, though, as you will see that's not always the case.

Actually, what we are under the control of in a threatening situation is the *feeling* of threat. It's the feeling that one is threatened which produces the physiological responses called "emotion."

Comedian Bob Newhart is among the many persons who are fearful of airline travel. For him, any flight in a plane is a "white knuckle" trip.

Certainly there isn't anything about an airplane which is intrinsically threatening. Mr. Newhart wouldn't say, "That airplane is out to get me!" Nor is there anything about flying which in itself is threatening. It's the notion—the feeling—that the plane might stop flying when it isn't supposed to that produces the fear. More directly, it's the impending sudden stop.

Most people who travel by air don't experience the kind of fear that Bob Newhart does, or they are able to control their fear. In part, what makes that possible is that they are optimistic about the plane continuing to remain airborne until its scheduled landing, and also the fact that they are not constantly aware that they are flying.

I travel by plane with some frequency, and I am (still) among those who feel comfortable when I do so. But on a trip from Los Angeles to Sacramento, I learned how rapidly comfort can turn to fear. Without warning, the pilot put the Boeing 707 into a steep dive to avoid a small aircraft. During that dive I simultaneously lost my optimism and immediately became conscious that I was flying. A few seconds and three thousand feet later, once the plane was flying straight and level, I became aware of the emotional state my feeling of fear had aroused. I discovered I am not an eternal optimist.

As for those who may truly always be the optimist, there is a story about a window washer who was working on the twenty-fifth floor of a skyscraper. A gust of wind caught his scaffold, tipping it at a forty-five degree angle. In the process, the window washer lost his footing and fell off. As he plummeted past the fifteenth floor, a tenant in one of the offices who was standing at an open window heard him say, "So far, so good!"

The problem with trying to resolve the chicken-and-egg dilemma with regard to feelings and emotions is that there isn't necessarily a clear-cut cause-effect relationship. Some psychologists say it isn't simply a matter of experiencing a particular feeling, which then causes a set of bodily responses. Recent theory has it that there's a vicious circle: feelings beget emotions, which in turn set the stage for more of the feelings which produced them.

If you find yourself in a situation in which you feel inadequate, proportionate to the feeling of inadequacy, the usual physiological changes occur. Because these changes interfere with your ability to function adequately, you feel even more inadequate.

For example, imagine that you are a professional baseball player. All your experience has been in the minor leagues. One day while you're playing in a game, the major league scout decides you're ready for the big time.

The very next day you're scheduled to pitch to some of the heaviest hitters in the league. You don't think you're ready. You feel inadequate to the assignment. The emotion or bodily state which your feeling of inadequacy produces is so extreme that you are virtually paralyzed. As a result, your pitching is terrible and as batter after batter scores a hit, your feeling that you are inadequate is confirmed.

Feelings, then, are your expression or description of how you see your relationship to specific situations. Each of us seeks to be adequate in whatever situation faces us. Any feeling other than adequacy causes disequilibrium, and it's our human condition that we strive for balance. Where a situation produces tension, we strive to reduce the tension.

A simple demonstration of tension reduction is one which most of us have experienced. Try it on someone else and watch the reaction. Stare at another person's nose while you're talking with him. Before long that person will either rub his nose surreptitiously or will get out a handkerchief.

The staring makes the other person imagine that there is something about the condition of his nose which is not acceptable. He is inadequate in the social situation at that moment. His behavior is directed toward becoming adequate.

In the same way, whatever feeling you have other than adequacy is accompanied by an emotional state which is a part of the striving for adequacy. It's a combination of a recognition (feeling) that there's a need to take action, and the physical readiness to do so (emotion).

For example, if your child strikes another, it is likely that he feels a need to enhance his perception that he is equal to his peer in terms of physical strength or courage, or the fact that he feels threatened, which causes him to do so. In either case, the greater his perceived need (feeling), the stronger his emotional reaction. A child doesn't hit because he feels angry; he hits because he feels a need to do so and his accompanying bodily state has prepared him for the action.

For some children, examinations are merely another part of school. They are to be expected periodically, and when they come, they're just something else that has to be done. For other children, they're a traumatic event on which their entire future depends. To the first group of children, an examination is a measure of the quality of the teaching/learning process. To the second group, an examination is an evaluation of them.

The difference is in the degree of personal reference. It's much the same as the entertainer who appears so relaxed on stage. He perceives himself as one who is there to make the audience "feel good." In contrast, a person who suffers from stage fright does so because he is concentrating on himself. In effect, perceiving his relationship to the situation as one in which the audience is there to make *him* feel good.

One of the phases in training to become a counselor is supervised practice. Through the counselor education department at the college or university, the would-be counselor is put in contact with individuals who feel the need for counseling.

The counselee is aware that he is dealing with a student, which puts the counselor under some tension. But even more tension is generated when the sessions are viewed by other counseling students and/or by the instructor.

Generally the first few sessions are very tense as the counselor, his mind on himself rather than his client, tries consciously to play the role he believes is expected of him. He has observed professional counselors and has read all the textbooks, so he has an idea that a counselor is supposed to have a certain look about him as he "does his thing."

The result of all this tension is that his ability to listen—the very reason he's there with the counselee—becomes practically nonexistent. There's a lesson for parents in that paradox.

When your child is under tension, his ability to listen to you is reduced. The greater the tension, the less likely you are to get your messages across. The trick is to help him get his mind off himself. For example, if your child has behaved in an unacceptable manner and you have found out about it, a confrontation will be tension-producing. Help your child work through the tension by acknowledging it. Only when the tension is past can you teach him that there is an acceptable alternative to his behavior.

Children feel tense either because they have a need to maintain their perception of what they are physically and psychologically, or because they have a need to enhance that perception.

A child who steals toys from a store gives them to other children. Why does he do so? It isn't clear from that tiny bit of information, of course, precisely what his self-concept is relative to other children. If the others are bigger, perhaps he feels threatened by them and attempts to buy their friendship, thus reducing the threat. If he perceives himself as a popular child on the basis of his parents' messages and is actually disliked by these other children, maybe he's trying to enhance his self-concept. In any case, however, his behavior is designed to make him feel adequate, and to reduce the tension which accompanies his not feeling so.

If your child lies to you, it's because he fears the truth will result in punishment—will cause you to react to him in a different way than usual—or because he fears his own perception of himself will be rejected by you. Here again, he seeks to remain adequate.

Psychologists Arthur W. Combs and Donald Snygg state that "The degree of emotion or tension experienced by the individual will be roughly proportional to the perceived importance of the relationship of the event to the self."[1]

In other words, if Sally witnesses Johnny being spanked by the principal, Sally is somewhat disturbed because

---

[1] Arthur W. Combs and Donald Syngg, *Individual Behavior*, New York, Harper & Brothers, 1959, p. 229.

physical violence frightens her. Her parents do not believe in spanking. But if *she* is sent to the principal to be spanked, her tension will be much greater than it was when Johnny was the victim.

I recall the mother who told the teacher at the beginning of the year that her child was very sensitive and cried readily. She said, "If Maria does something wrong, just scold the child who sits next to her and Maria will behave."

Emotions, then, are bodily states which accompany feelings. Feelings are statements of how we perceive ourselves, how we perceive the situations in which we're involved and how these two are interrelated.

We make our feelings known to others by way of what might be called verbal shorthand. Certainly the words "I love you" aren't sufficient to convey the full experience of the feeling of being in love. Moreover, the experience of being in love may not be the same for you as it is for me. But nevertheless we have agreed upon symbolic representations for the wide variety of our perceptions.

The stronger the feeling, the less able we are to convey it to others. Thus, "He makes me so angry I can't describe it!" But at the same time, the stronger the feeling, the more conscious we are of our bodily state, and the less able we are to conceal the feeling.

We have seen that whatever one perceives in a situation involves his bodily state. It follows, then, that when one describes how he feels, for the most part he is describing his awareness of his bodily state or emotion at the time.

If you say, "I'm anxious about going to the dentist this afternoon," you are actually describing your perception of your bodily state. But it's only because we agree as to what kinds of things make up the bodily state, or emotion, which accompanies the feeling of anxiety that I understand to some degree how you feel. If I say, "What do you mean by anxious?", you might say, "It feels as though there's a tightness in my stomach."

In the same situation, your small child, lacking the language skill to describe how he feels about going to the dentist, may just refuse, saying, "I don't feel like going," or

"I don't want to go." His resistance is then assumed to be generated by willful disobedience rather than by anxiety.

Feelings and emotions always occur together. Intense feelings are accompanied by intense emotions and vice versa. But there are situations in which emotions are so strong that only later is there an awareness of how one felt at the time.

For example, if your life is threatened, all the bodily conditions—acceleration of physiological systems—necessary for your survival are heightened. Not until the threat is past do you become aware of how frightened you were. The reason for this, of course, is that feelings are your descriptions of your bodily state. When your life is threatened, you don't stop to assess and describe your bodily state.

This means that it isn't necessary to know how you feel in order to act. Behavior is not the result of feeling, it's the result of the totality of your perception. Thus if you are about to be run down by an automobile, you don't stop to describe your body's mobilization for flight. You perceive instantly that your "self" is in immediate danger of death or serious injury and you act to save yourself. This is as true for children as it is for adults.

All behavior is the product of the total organism. If your child acts in a way which seems to indicate an absence of thought, that's a deception. Feelings don't produce behavior. And they don't occur in the absence of thought.

If your child does something unacceptable, don't excuse the behavior by saying, "He didn't know what he was doing because he was so upset." The fact is, he acted because he perceived a need to do so in order to relieve tension. The idea that he was upset is actually a description of the tension, and is more than likely *your* description rather than your child's.

By the same token, you can believe your child if he says he lied to you because he was afraid to tell the truth. For example, suppose you came home to find your beautiful cut crystal pitcher in pieces. Your child denied any knowledge of what happened and said that the cat must have done it.

Later you discovered that your child did break the pitcher by throwing a football. You are angry because the damage was done and even angrier because you were lied to.

"Why didn't you tell me the truth when I asked you?"

"I was afraid to."

The lie was a means of reducing tension. As your child perceived the situation, telling the truth would mean immediate threat to his "self". By lying, he placed psychological distance (time) between himself and the threat.

Some school children put off studying until they are faced with a test. For some a test is a means of enhancing their self-perception, for others it is a threat to their self perception. In either case, preparation is delayed until tension is increased by the immediacy of the test. The more immediate, the more frantic the studying.

To sum up, then, emotion is the speeding up of the body's functions so that there is sufficient energy to cope with the demands with which we are faced. The greater the demand, the greater the physiological acceleration.

Feeling is one's description of what a particular situation or event means to him. It tells about one's perception of the interaction between himself and the situation or event.

Counselors Donald and Nancy Tubesing state that the distinction between communication through thinking and communication through feeling "is not in the label 'I feel' or 'I think,' but in the essence of what's being communicated."[2] We're going to explore that concept in the next few pages.

Let's do some more supposing. This time, that you are asked to be the president of the parent-teacher group at your child's school. You are flattered, but you say, "I appreciate being asked, but I just don't feel I can spare the time."

What you really mean is, "I don't *think* I can spare the

---

[2] Donald A. and Nancy L. Tubesing, *Tune In*, Milwaukee, Wisconsin, Listening Group, 1973, p. 29.

time." You may *feel* pressured because of the demands of your business enterprise. You may *feel* anxious that you won't be able to meet the next payment on that note with the bank. You may *feel* uncomfortable about working with Bill Smith, who is a member of the group. All those things may cause you to think you won't have the time to accept the presidency. "Pressured," "anxious" and "uncomfortable" are feelings. "I can't spare the time," is not a feeling.

As a general rule, if you can precede what you believe to be a feeling with the words, "I am," you have identified a feeling. This is true for other tenses of the verb "to be" also (I was, I will be, etc.).

One reason it's important for you to know the difference between thoughts and feelings is that your child doesn't or at least he can't tell you. If some problem at school causes him to say, "I don't like Mrs. Smith (the teacher)," does he mean, "I think Mrs. Smith doesn't like me," or does he mean, "I feel put down by Mrs. Smith and I don't like to feel put down."?

Another reason you should know how to distinguish thought and feeling is to make your communications to your child more clear. For instance, you can say, "I think you should be punished because you were a bad girl (or boy) for doing what you did," or you can say, "I am unhappy that you did this. Because you knew you were not supposed to, you will have to do thus and so (naming the punishment)."

Still a third reason for knowing the difference between thoughts and feelings is to help your child make his communications clear. For example, if he says, "I'm going to kill that old Mr. Higgens!", your impulse is to respond with something like, "Now you know you don't mean that!" If that's your response, your child won't listen to you. Right at that very moment, he really has strong feelings which he is unable to share. That tension we talked about earlier must be reduced first. So if you want to get his ear, and if you want him to tell you what has aroused those feelings, you say, "It sounds as though something happened between you and Mr. Higgins that has made you very angry."

We'll get into the kinds of techniques you can use to encourage your child to listen and to share his feelings in the next chapter. Right now, let's do a little work on identifying and distinguishing between thoughts and feelings.

Someone says to you, "I feel that you're angry because of what I did." Is that person sharing a thought or a feeling? If you remember the general rule, you will recognize that this is a thought. Unfortunately it's a poor statement not only because it doesn't share the speaker's feeling, but because the speaker has assumed that he knows how *you* feel. The speaker would be sharing *his* feelings if he said, "I'm concerned (or upset, or worried) that what I did might have made you angry." I'll leave it to you to decide how each of the two statements would affect you.

If you have difficulty getting your child out of bed in the morning and ready for school, you have probably heard the words, "I don't feel like going to school today." Do those words actually convey a feeling? Or do they convey a thought? How would you respond to the statement?

Your child knows that he would not get by with, "I think I will stay home from school today," or "I want to stay home from school today." So the words aren't intended to convey a thought. But they don't convey a feeling, either, if you apply the "I am" rule.

It's when your child comes up with this kind of statement that you must help him clarify how he feels. What he may be trying to tell you, but isn't skilled enough to do so on his own, is something like, "Mr. Brown is having a math test today. I'm afraid to take it because I haven't studied. If I stay home, I won't have to take the test." That comes out as, "I don't feel like going to school today."

Here's another situation. Your little daughter comes into the house after playing outside. "I don't feel good," she announces. The thermometer is produced and discloses a normal temperature. "There can't be much wrong with you, dear, why don't you go outside and play with Susie?" "I don't want to play with Susie. She doesn't like me!"

What about it? Did the statement, "I don't feel good,"

convey a thought or a feeling? This is one of the cases where the "I am" rule doesn't work. But if you restate your daughter's words as, "I feel bad," you can see that this is a statement of feeling, however vague it may be. Such obscure and generalized feeling words are typical of young children's speech, because they don't have the kind of vocabulary to describe the nuances of feelings. Here again, some clarification on your part will bring communication dividends in terms of a sharing of deeper feelings.

So we now have a second rule in addition to the "I am" generalization. The statement "I feel," *when followed by a word that communicates a feeling* is a second way to determine whether an utterance is one of feeling rather than thought. Let's try a few of these. You determine which ones contain a statement of feeling. The correct answers are at the top of the next page.

1. "I have the distinct feeling that you're not comfortable with me."
2. "I don't like it when you say rotten things like that to me."
3. "I like my teacher, but he hates me. He didn't even answer me when I said, 'Good morning.' "
4. "The vice principal is so mean, he gave me a detention slip just because I was combing my hair in the cafeteria. Then he made me stand and finish my lunch. I was so embarrassed!"
5. "Eleanor did that deliberately and I'm furious with her."
6. "I'm not at all sure that this will work out for either of us."
7. "Goodness knows I can stand improvement. It's just that I felt Walter should have come to *me* with his complaints."
8. "I'm fed up with your behavior, young man!"
9. "I have the feeling that you're not telling me the truth."
10. "I feel that you have betrayed my trust in you by leaving the house when you promised not to."

Numbers 4, 5, 6, 8 and 10 contain statements of feeling. Here's how to read them:

4. "I was embarrassed."
5. "I'm furious."
6. "I'm not sure." (I'm unsure.)
8. "I'm fed up."
10. "I feel betrayed."

Now, using the "I am" rule and the "I feel" rule, go back and write each of the statements of thought as a statement of feeling. I've included some possible responses below. They aren't by any means offered as examples of ideal responses. See what you can do, then meet me back here.

1. "I feel uncomfortable with you, because I think you're uncomfortable with me."
2. "I am upset by your behavior toward me."
3. "I feel rejected by my teacher."
7. "I'm hurt that Walter criticized me to other people."
9. "I'm disturbed because I think you're lying to me."

How did you do? Do you see the difference between telling someone how and what you feel and telling them what's on your mind?

Let's try a few more for practice. First decide which of the statements below convey feelings (the answers are at the top of the next page), then rewrite the thought statements as feeling statements.

1. "It's hard to believe you could work that fast."
2. "After those conflicting statements, I'm thoroughly confused."
3. "I guess if there's no way to avoid it, I'll have to face the music."
4. "I couldn't be more disconsolate over the situation."
5. "I feel he's too shy to ask her. It couldn't be anything else."
6. "That was a boring course. I slept through most of it."

7. "Contempt of court? Sure, the court is contemptible. I feel I got a raw deal!"

Numbers 2 and 4 are feeling statements.

Following are examples of how to change the statements of thought above, to statements of feeling.

1. "I'm skeptical about your claim."
3. "I'm resigned."
5. "I'm convinced that he's too shy to ask her."
6. "I was bored."
7. "I am frustrated by the judge's decision. I think it's unjustified."

You should have the idea now. Next time your child tries to use a tall story to get off the hook, I hope you won't say, "I think you're lying," but instead will state your feeling: "I'm not convinced," or "I'm unsure of the truth of what you're telling me." More importantly, I hope you're sensitized enough so that you can see the difference between the two kinds of statements and the effect each would have on your child's willingness to listen.

Let's proceed now with the third objective of this chapter, which is to enable you to tell the difference between an *expression* of feeling and a *description* of feeling.

When I use the words "expression of feeling," I mean any of a variety of ways by which we let another person know what we are feeling. All fall in the general classification, "language."

Language can be of two types. We can use words, as we have been doing in this book—in other words, verbal language. Or we can use nonverbal or body language, such as a raised eyebrow, a shrug of the shoulders, a nod of the head, and so on. We're not going to go into detail about body language here. There are excellent books on the subject if you care to explore further. What we're concerned with are the problems that result when one's verbal and nonverbal language don't match.

A description of feeling, unlike an expression of feeling,

involves only verbal language. Nonverbal language has no part in a description of feelings. I know this gets a little sticky, so let me explain in more detail.

If, as an example, you say to your child, "Go to your room!", that's an *expression* of your feelings. If another driver nearly forces you off the road, your words of advice to him even though lost because of other noises and/or closed windows, might be something like, "Why don't you watch what you're doing! You stupid—!" That too is an expression of your feelings.

Now let's compare those reactions with descriptions of your feelings in the same situations. Instead of telling your child, "Go to your room," you say, "I asked you to pick up your toys. I am angry because they are not picked up." Your words, "I am angry," describe your feelings.

In the case of the inconsiderate and imprudent driver, there was no way, short of shouting (and you probably wouldn't be heard by the target of your verbal barrage), to describe adequately your feelings toward him. Your words might be something such as, "Your stupidity makes me mad as hell, and I'd like to punch you out!"

Here's another example. When you return home from an evening at the theater or a dinner date with friends, the babysitter greets you with a long list of your child's misbehaviors during the evening.

Next morning, little Arthur is met by stony cold silence at the breakfast table. The silence itself is an expression of feelings. Being a normal boy, Arthur is confused. He doesn't know quite how to react to silence. Next he's told, "Listen carefully, young man, because I'm not going to say this again! When you come home from school this afternoon, you will not go out to play. You will go straight to your room until dinner. You will not play with your toys. You will do your homework. Then you will go to bed." This again is an expression of feelings. Not only does it conceal the reason for your silent treatment of your son, it gives a set of directions which are probably beyond his ability to comprehend, remember and follow.

Here's the alternative, a description of your feelings. When Arthur comes down to breakfast, you say, "The babysitter told us that you disobeyed her last night. You took the dog into the bathtub with you, and you used mother's shampoo to give him a bath. You broke the lamp on your bed table when you played trampoline, and the cat is still trying to lick the peanut butter off his tail. We are very angry that you did not do as you were told." Having explained what he did, and having described how you feel about it, you can then decide on the consequences.

Your sixth grader returns from school with his report card. You note that he has A's and B's in his other subjects but in math his grade is D. He can see by the expression on your face that you are not satisfied. Not wishing to discourage him, you congratulate him on his A's and B's and, trying to ignore the one poor grade, make no mention of the D. You are surprised when he accepts your congratulations half-heartedly.

Whether you wanted to or not, your face provided a clear expression of your displeasure over the D. What you didn't know was that your child hasn't done a single one of the homework assignments for the quarter. He expected the poor grade and he expected that you would scold him for it. Your congratulations, or verbal expression, of your feelings didn't match. He's not sure which to believe. How much better it would have been if you had said, "You must be pleased with your grades in (science, reading, etc.). I'll have to admit that your grade in math perplexes me. How do you feel about it?"

The statement, "I'm perplexed by your grade in math," is congruent with, or matched, your nonverbal expression of disappointment. Moreover, it's consistent with the reaction your child expected.

Children begin very early in their lives to give messages which are not congruent. There are several reasons for this, including the example set by their parents and their need to defend their self concept. But the reason your child sends messages in which his expressed and described feelings are at odds is less important than the limitation this places on his ability to communicate clearly.

"Your teacher says that you have been causing a lot of

trouble at school. She called me today to let me know that you are not allowed to eat in the cafeteria. She said that last week she had to send you to the office every afternoon. What do you have to say for yourself?"

"Nothing," mouth downturned, eyes fixed on the floor.

"The principal said that he might put you in a different classroom. Your teacher says she is afraid she won't be able to keep you in her room if this continues. Do you want to go to another teacher? Please look at me when I talk to you!"

"Sure. I don't like old Mrs. Grace anyway. I'll be glad to get out of her crummy room!" Still staring at the floor.

"I told you to look at me." You put your hand beneath his chin.

"Very well, then. I'll call Mr. Strong, the principal, and tell him to put you with another teacher." You feel his tears falling on your wrist.

"I said to go ahead, what do I care!" Sobbing, he bolts from the room.

The boy's macho declaration that he would be glad to get out of Mrs. Grace's room was a description of feeling that was belied by his nonverbal behavior. Actually he wanted desperately to have Mrs. Grace like him and he wanted her to want him in her class. If this had been your child, what would have been your reaction? Would you have believed his words, or would you have trusted his body language? One thing is certain. The boy didn't have a prayer of solving his problem under the circumstances because he didn't, or couldn't, describe his feelings.

In Chapter Nine we talked about feelings and emotions. We said that feelings are our descriptions of how we see the interrelationships we have with our environment and with other people. Emotions, on the other hand, are the bodily states which accompany feelings and prepare us to take whatever action is needed to survive, or enhance, or protect our self-concept.

Next, we examined the difference between thoughts and feelings. Thoughts are located in the brain and are conveyed as conceptual or factual information. Feelings are, as already stated, our personal perceptions of our relationship to specific situations.

Finally, we discussed the distinction between expressions of feelings and descriptions of them. Feelings may be expressed either through verbal language or through nonverbal, or body language. Descriptions of feelings, however, must be given through the medium of words. When expressions and descriptions of feelings are not congruent, the message is open to confusion. But body language is usually a more reliable indicator of feeling.

In Chapter Ten we are going to take a look at your emotional constant. By that I mean the way you typically react to your child's descriptions and expressions of feelings. You will use that knowledge to help your child learn to be a good listener.

Chapter 10

In other words . . .

BEFORE we begin our discussion of "In other words
. . ." I have a little task for you. We have to do this
now, because I don't want you to have prior access to any
of the secrets you'll learn about in Chapter Ten.

The task is a simple one. Here's all you have to do.
Briefly respond to the following statement. Do so just as if
I were standing there with you and said,

"This inflation is wiping me out! I'd sell everything and
move to some little corner of the world where life doesn't
cost an arm and a leg, but all those little corners seem to
be gone!"

All right, write your response and tuck it between the
pages of this book for future reference. You'll understand
later why I asked you to do it.

Now let's proceed. Chapter Ten contains a lot of very
useful information.

By now you realize that if you want to get your child to
listen to you, you have to know how to talk to him or her.
Of equal importance is the way *you* listen when your child
is attempting to communicate with you. A necessary com-
ponent in the listening process is your response, because
listening—real listening—is an active occupation.

After all, if your child talks to you, unless you respond
in some way, he has no way of knowing whether you
heard what he had to say. But the mere act of responding

isn't sufficient to keep the conversational ball rolling. The way you respond has an effect. Depending on the type of response, you may enhance the communication process or you may completely turn off your child. If he sees that you don't listen to him, he won't listen to you. He will *learn* not to listen.

Each of us, to some extent, has developed a peculiar way of providing "feedback" to our children (and to other adults), a sort of characteristic style of response. Elias Porter has identified some major kinds of responses: advice-giving, probing, supportive, interpretive and paraphrasing.[1]

At times we employ each of the different responses because there are occasions when each is appropriate. Generally, though, we confine ourselves to two or perhaps three of them. Because of the effect the different response styles have on communications with our children, we are going to examine each in detail. Your objective will be to identify your own response style. Knowing how you generally respond to your child will enable you to determine whether you are turning him off. If so, your awareness that you are will provide the medium through which you can begin to change so that you can turn him on instead.

Are you an *Advice Giver?* Advice givers seem to have a need to make judgments about and evaluate their children's statements. Rather than assisting their children to examine alternatives and make rational decisions, advice givers indicate that they have all the answers. Only they are truly capable of making correct decisions as to what their children should do.

The biggest problem with advice-giving statements—ones which lead your child to believe there is only one right answer and that you have it—is this: the decisions your child will have to make about his life will not be that simple. To begin with, you won't be there at every turn to supply "the" answer. Your child will have to make choices regarding his actions and he will have to make them on his own. He will continually be asking himself, "What's

[1] Elias H. Porter, *An Introduction to Therapeutic Counseling*, Boston, Houghton Mifflin, 1950.

the thing for *me* to do right now, in this place, under these conditions?" Will he, for example, join the gang dropping acid because they tell him the answer is "Yes." Or will he be able to decide that for him the answer is, "No!"

Remember that at times you *must* make advice-giving responses. For example, you see that a certain course of action your child's statement informs you he is going to take will be injurious or illegal. You certainly would not stand back and allow him to do what he plans to in those circumstances, and there may not be time to analyze the situation cooperatively with him.

Here's an example of an advice-giving response:

Your daughter says, "Betsy thinks she's so smart! She got the only "A" on the history test today. I know she cheated, because I saw her peek in her book and get the answers!"

"What you ought to do is go and tell your teacher. It isn't right for someone to cheat and get away with it."

Here's another example:

"Bobby said all the other kids could come over and see his new puppy, but he didn't invite me."

"I'd just go over there anyway."

Those are advice-giving responses. Do they characterize you?

Maybe you're a *Prober*. A probing response style makes the user sound like Melvin Belli. It's almost a cross-examination. A major difficulty with probing responses is that they direct the conversation toward your interests and away from your child's. The prober seeks clarification of what the other person said, and that's OK, except that the clarification is for the prober's and not the speaker's benefit.

Probing responses can help *you* understand how your child feels, but they don't help your child to understand *his* feelings better. Finally, probing responses limit your child to the aspect of his statement you're interested in, or even worse, may completely change the subject, leaving your child and his feeling twisting slowly in the breeze, while the communication process disintegrates.

Probing responses sound like this:

"I tore my arithmetic paper today and Mr. Frile made me stay after school. I . . ."

"What did you expect him to do? You know better than to tear your paper. What were you thinking of?"

"Aw, forget it!"

"Don't you talk to me that way, young man! You can go to your room for the rest of the evening."

What your child was about to share with you was the information that he tore his paper by accident. Mr. Frile didn't let him explain either, and just punished him. Your child is hurt, because he likes Mr. Frile, and because he was unfairly punished by him.

To add to the problem, he is now hurt by your insensitivity. He loves you, but you punished him unfairly also, and wouldn't let him share with you how he felt. Moreover, you misconstrue his, "Aw, forget it!" to be a defiant gesture.

Another probing response, less damaging, but just as unproductive goes like this:

"A bunch of the guys are going skiing this weekend," your daughter announces excitedly. "Carol's folks have this neat lodge up at Bear Mountain. They said she could use it. Carol invited me. Can I go? Please!"

"Who is this 'bunch of guys' who are going?"

"You know, just the regular crowd I go with."

"Are there going to be both boys and girls?"

"Well, yeah, but Carol's aunt is going to chaperone, and . . ."

"I don't know Carol's aunt. How old is she? Is she married?"

And so it goes, ad nauseum, almost to the point where the child believes it isn't worth all the questioning.

How do you feel about *Supportive* responses? Are they your style? Those who habitually use supportive responses have the best of intentions, but in terms of sharing feelings, perhaps the worst effect.

We talked about permitting your child to "own" his feelings. The supportive response doesn't leave room for that. It says, in effect, that his feeling isn't at all unique, that everybody, or almost everybody has felt that way. It falls just a little short of saying to your child, "You don't really feel that way at all."

Here's how the supportive response looks in action:

"Mom, I thought for sure that Robert would ask me to go to the senior prom. I'm so miserable I could die!"

"There, there, dear, it's not that bad, lots of girls have had the same experience. You're still a sophomore, and there'll be other chances. I remember my first prom. There was a boy who . . ."

Another supportive response is quite commonly used with small children. It goes like this:

Your five year old arrives from school, crying.

"Mommy, Jimmy tore my dress when we got off the bus (sob) and he told me I was stupid, n' . . ."

"Oh, you poor child! Come here, dear and stop crying. I'm sure Jimmy didn't mean what he said. Just let me dry your eyes, and go and change your clothes. You'll feel better after you've had a glass of milk and some cookies."

If you don't fall in any of the foregoing categories, maybe you tend toward *Interpretive* responses. The interpretive response is first cousin to the probing response. It goes a step further, however.

The prober seeks information to clarify the child's statement for himself, and that's the end of it. But the interpreter wants the information for another purpose. He draws conclusions about his own feeling with regard to his child's statement, and then, based on those conclusions, explains to the child how he feels. Or he draws conclusions about his own thoughts concerning his child's statement so that he can describe his child's thoughts to him.

Interpretive responses follow this general line:

"I'm sick of little brothers and sisters! I wish I didn't have any. Only children sure are lucky!"

"When I was your age I said the same thing. The reason you feel that way is because you're growing up and you'd like to have some privacy. Only children are lucky because they usually have their own room. You're thinking that you'd like that."

Still another example of the interpretive response:

"I know I'll probably get in trouble with Mrs. Proust, but I'm just not in the mood this weekend to write a paper for her English Lit. class."

"I'd feel that way too, dear, if I were as tired as you are. You can't expect to feel like writing anything after working all day at the store. Get a good night's sleep and you'll feel better about it tomorrow."

The last response style, *Paraphrasing*, is at the same time best to use and the least used of the five. The greatest virtue of the paraphrase is that it permits you to be sure that what you heard is what your child intended you to.

Most of the difficulty you have when you communicate with your child probably comes from one source: inference. You must be sure that your responses and reactions to your child's messages—verbal or nonverbal—are based on accurate understanding of what he said.

There's only one way you can be sure they are. Ask.

When I say ask, I don't mean in the sense of a probing response. This is a different kind of question. It invites a give-and-take. When effectively used, the paraphrasing response helps your child understand what he means and how he feels even better than he did initially. Let's see what paraphrase looks like in action.

"Mom! Mom! Guess what? I get to be the principal's messenger next week! Only the kids with the best grades get to be that. I hope I do it right. I can hardly wait until dad gets home!"

"It sounds like you're really excited about being chosen. You seem proud, but anxious too, about having all that responsibility."

That's a fairly high-level paraphrase. Here's an example of one at a somewhat lower level. We'll go into detail about the different levels in the next chapter.

"Mom, why is dad always on my back? I try to do what I'm supposed to around the house, but it never seems to be right. It gets to where I don't even feel like trying anymore!"

"If I heard you correctly, you're telling me that you and

your father don't agree on standards for the work you've been assigned. Is that right?"

"Well, not exactly. I'd be happy to do things just the way dad says he wants them done, and I try to. But he's always demanding more, like it's some kind of game where I never know the rules."

"Are you saying that your father keeps changing the standards without telling you beforehand, as though he wants to find something to criticize you for?"

"Yeah, that's more like it. I think he actually *wants* me not to please him."

And so it goes. It's a continuing process of statement, request for clarification, feedback, restatement, request for further clarification, feedback, and so on, until both parties are satisfied that they have the same understanding of the message.

At the lowest level, paraphrase is a pure restatement: "My name is Harry Brown."

"Did you say Harry Brown?"

"Right."

Were you able to identify your personal style or styles of responding to your child? More to the point, do you now have a better idea of how your response style may be causing a communication breakdown between you and your child?

In just a moment you're going to do a little work to sharpen up your ability to identify response styles. But first, under the heading of unfinished business, remember the statement I asked you to respond to at the beginning of this chapter? Get it out now, and look at your response. What style did you use? Would you still respond the same way now? If you say, "Yes," congratulations! Go to the head of the class. Chances are you communicate so well with your child that you don't need this book. If you said, "No," then let's proceed.

I'm going to do the lion's share of the first of two exercises. Here are some responses to statements. See if you can identify the style of each: advice, probe, support, interpretation, or paraphrase.

1. I know just how you feel. Goodness knows that when I was your age . . .
2. Given your situation, here's what I'd do.
3. Don't let it worry you, son.
4. Did you try telling him to give the job to someone more familiar with the town? Why didn't you speak up?
5. It's certainly easy to understand why you'd have that opinion. After all, you got the best marks, and . . .
6. Anyone in your position ought to make an example of that sort of behavior.
7. Unless I'm mistaken, you're quite concerned about making the team again this year. Or have I missed the point of what you were saying?
8. Why did you stand for that kind of insult? How could you let that lump talk to you like that?
9. Now there's no use in carrying on like that. Tomorrow it will all be forgotten. Just you wait and see.
10. You're really bugged by all this, it seems to me. It sounds as though you're thinking of leaving college.

Were you able to figure out where each of those ten responses belongs? The answers follow so you can check out *your* perceptions. I hope you get a perfect score. Rate yourself 3 or less correct, stone-cold; 4 to 6 correct, cool; 7 to 8 correct, lukewarm; 9 to 10, a born counselor.

Here are the styles represented in the responses: 1. Support 2. Advice 3. Support 4. Probe 5. Interpretation 6. Advice 7. Paraphrase 8. Probe 9. Support 10. Paraphrase

This time you do the work while I sit back and listen. Here's what I'd like you to do. In response to the following statement, write a response which fits each of the five styles: advice-giving, probing, supporting, interpreting, and paraphrasing. Here's the statement:

"You know, dad, everybody in that class hates me just because I get the top grades. I don't have anybody I can talk to in the whole bunch. The whole thing really has me down."

O.K., go to it. Some possible responses follow but don't peek until you've written some of your own.

Advice: "Tell you what I'd do, son. I'd take a page from old Ben Franklin's book, and ask one of the most popular people in the class to do you a favor. For instance . . ."

Probing: "Why would they all feel that way about you? Do they have some idea that you're not getting those marks honestly?"

Support: "Don't let it get you down, son. It's not as if you're going to have to live with those kids the rest of your life. Besides, I'd be willing to bet that most good students have the same experience."

Interpretation: "I expect that the reason you're having that kind of problem is only indirectly related to your grades. It's probably the fact that you spend so much time with your nose in your books that has made you feel isolated. You attribute your isolation to your classmates."

Paraphrase: "It sounds like your lack of popularity has you more concerned than the drive to get top grades. Right at this point you'd gladly trade a few good grades for a few friends."

If you had trouble writing the various styles of response, some review is necessary. Go back and read the chapter again. Remember that your objective is to identify your own characteristic response style so that ultimately you may change it if necessary. Assuming that you have met that objective, I want to encourage you to dig a little deeper into your personality. Your second objective in this chapter is to find out how you feel about feelings—yours and others.

What we're going to do now is to see what kinds of connections exist between your typical manner of responding to the statements of others, and your personality. What kind of person, for example, typically adopts the stance of advice-giver, of prober, of supporter, etc.?

We have seen that as children we become programmed through our interactions with our parents, relatives, significant adults and others, to handle our feelings, and those of others, in characteristic ways. We have observed, for instance, that a boy whose father needs to be seen as the "he-man" or "macho" type may have difficulty expressing his love for that father by hugging or kissing him. It is traditional in our American society that men do not hug and kiss one another. They shake hands to demonstrate affection.

We know also that as children we learned that certain kinds of feelings are permissible and others are not. We mentioned, for example, that most people have difficulty dealing with strong feelings. Anger is a no-no and love is for sissies or girls, not for boys. These are not universals, of course, and your own life experiences have determined your typical reactions to feeling-producing situations.

Reactions have been grouped in two major classes: those which permit "tough feelings" and those which permit "tender feelings." Individuals who are in the group which permit tough feelings do not permit tender feelings. Conversely, those who are grouped with the ones who permit tender feelings don't permit tough feelings.

Within these two major groups there have been identified four feeling styles: the "nice guy," who accepts tender feelings but rejects tough feelings; the "achiever, who accepts tough feelings, but rejects tender ones; the "logical thinker," who doesn't accept either tough or tender feelings; the "authentic person," who is totally accepting and open to all kinds of feelings.[2]

According to the situation in which persons belonging to each of these feeling style groups find themselves, they will demonstrate typical kinds of behaviors. Let's see what this means as far as your responses to your child are concerned.

If you're a *nice guy*, your main concern will be to avoid any exaggeration of angry feelings. Mother frequently adopts the nice guy role. If the children are engaged in a dispute, she immediately directs her attention to ending the disharmony, even making irrational concessions in order to accomplish that goal. In effect, she will do anything "to keep peace in the family."

The nice guy parent is walked all over by his child. He

[2] Donald A. and Nancy L. Tubesing, *Tune In*, Milwaukee, Wisconsin, Listening Group, 1973, p. 44.

is willing to accept that, though, in order to avoid being disliked or rejected by the child. He is forever laying himself down to bridge whatever troubled domestic or parental waters he encounters. If he can't bridge them, he pours liberal volumes of soothing oil on them. He can't say, "No" to his child.

Nice guys are given to praising their children rather than encouraging them, to placating them rather than standing ground and sticking with principles. The nice guy is also an inveterate gift-giver who both overindulges with material goods and showers attention. When his child does not respond by doing what he is expected to, the typical reaction is "How could you do that to me after all I've done for you?"

The nice guy has much difficulty communicating with his child. Because he fears hostile feelings, he doesn't listen to his child's descriptions of them. He doesn't want to hear them. When his child's behavior evokes feelings of anger on his part, he is unable to share them with his child.

If you're a nice guy parent, there's something you can do to help yourself. Become more assertive. There are courses which assist in that direction and, of course, there are books which you can read, such as *When I Say No, I Feel Guilty.*

Achievers love to manage their children's lives. They have the kids running in all directions: music lessons, dance lessons, scouting, etc., etc. They demand performance. If their child belongs to any group, it has to be in a leadership role. If he belongs to a team, they'd better win. At school they are critical of the teacher who doesn't assign homework. Their children must get top grades.

Only recently has our society permitted women to join the achiever group. In the past, achievers have been men. Organizers, decision-makers, movers-and-shakers were almost exclusively males. Women have now infiltrated those ranks. What used to be called "ambition," "drive," when men were being described, is now identified in women as "aggression," or being "pushy."

I mention that only by way of indicating that the acceptance of tough feelings and the rejection of tender feelings is no longer a male characteristic. Women too display that aspect of the achiever. A friend recently observed that we haven't come so far in our move toward sexual equality in the job marketplace that women still don't have to pay a price for success in that male arena. He believes that the price is femininity. If the inability to deal with tender feelings marks a loss of femininity, perhaps my friend is correct.

Achievers love power and one of their greatest fears is losing it. They have a need to dominate their children's lives not only in terms of the activities we've already mentioned, but in other, more important respects: career choice, selection of a marriage partner, even when and how many children they should have. It's not necessarily that there's any sentimentality in their wanting grandchildren; they may merely want to serve as the catalyst for procreation.

A lot of the manipulation of his child which is so dear to the heart of the achiever is accomplished through destructive and dangerous means: threat of reprisal or denial of affection. It is typical of the achiever to say such things as, "Unless you finish college before you get married, you're no child of mine," or "If you marry that girl, I don't ever want to see you again," or "If you insist on becoming a member of that religion, I'll cut you out of my will."

Achievers are given to impulse, something which often causes problems with their parenting functions. For one thing, they select punishments which turn out to be more punishing to them than to their children. For example, "You were told to come home from Morton's house at four-thirty. Because you were late, from now on your friends will have to come over here to play." Great! Mom is now stuck with the entire tribe until she conveniently manages to forget that impulsively formulated rule.

Want to know what you should do if you're an achiever? Like the nice guy, take pride in your good points—your competitive spirit and your gift for organization—but accept the fact that you're impatient and illogical. You can't will yourself to change those traits, but your awareness of them is a beginning. If you accept and remain aware, change will occur.

Might you be a *logical thinker?* The logical thinker operates with almost computer-like precison. Information is solicited and analyzed and recommendations of others are carefully weighed and evaluated by the logical thinker. He is the parent who has a habit of explaining his child's explanations, often beginning with the words, "What you're trying to say is . . ." or "What you actually mean is . . ."

The logical thinker often reaches the executive ranks because he *is* a clear thinker. But he often is stalled in his progress up the corporate ladder because he is abrasive in his criticism and is foolish enough to aim it at his superiors as well as those he supervises. He treats his family in precisely the same way.

Because he is pretty much an automaton, feelings are not a part of his daily life. He rejects both strong and tender feelings in others and does not permit them of himself. If someone does happen to penetrate his "feeling armor," he is aware of them in himself and in others and can deal a "strong" person on the individual who has gotten to him. He may say something such as, "I know you think I'm a strong person, but the truth is, I'm not."

The logical thinker must have everything in order. He is obsessed with systems for managing his home—and family. To get the order he must have, he tends to manipulate. His manipulation he assumes mistakenly to be a superior ability to lead. He pushes his child along paths which are determined for him.

The logical thinker infrequently will do another a favor. He does not believe in encouraging others, believing that whatever they do should be expected of them. By the same token he does not accept favors graciously. In fact he scarcely acknowledges them. Gifts are an embarrassment because they carry the implication that he is somehow indebted to the giver, and he does not like to owe anything to another.

In social situations he tends to try to impress others by demonstrating his intelligence and his gift for logical thinking. He also places a high value on intelligence when others display it. Everything the logical thinker does in his social life is "straight arrow" and he expects others, his children included, to behave in precisely the same fashion.

If you corner a logical thinker, he will withdraw and gather his intellectual and emotional resources. If there is any risk, he will go by the book because it's safer.

It isn't surprising that the logical thinker handles his interactions with his child the same way he does with adults. If there's a breach of behavior, he will ignore his child's feelings and deal only with facts, probing and evaluating them, for example. He will try to arrive at a conclusion as to who was right and who was wrong if another child is involved.

He does not permit his child to become intimate with him. He is as unable to tell his child how he feels as he is unable to deal with his child's feelings.

Obviously, if you happen to be the logical thinker type, you will need to become more accepting. You should work on becoming aware of feelings, being at least a bit more open, and learning how to describe your feelings.

There aren't very many around, but it's possible that you're one of the few *authentic persons*. The authentic or adequate person has a full repertoire of feelings and is free to select whichever of the feeling styles is appropriate to the situation.

The authentic person doesn't stifle others. He accepts them for what they are and does not have a need to mold them into his system. Because he is not afraid of feelings, he is aware of them in himself and in others and can deal with them constructively, using them as a medium of psychological growth.

The authentic or adequate person and Maslow's concept of the "self-actualized" person are one and the same; he is characteristically able to accept others and able to accept himself. Such a person is also open to all experiences. In Maslow's words, self-actualized individuals ". . . can accept their own human nature with all its shortcomings, with all its discrepancies from the ideal image, without feeling real concern . . . they can take the frailties and sins, weaknesses and evils of human nature in the same unquestioning spirit that one takes or accepts the characteristics of nature. One does not complain about water because it is wet, or about rocks because they are hard, or about trees because they are green."[3]

I want to say a word about accepting your child's behavior, but before I do a point needs to be clarified. Please don't confuse the idea of accepting your child's actions with liking or approving them. Acceptance means only that you acknowledge the fact that your child is not going to live up to your ideal image; that he is going to do things which you don't want him to. That's a "weakness of human nature," as Maslow puts it.

Another thing about acceptance is that one need not be completely self-actualized or totally authentic, whatever one defines "completely" or "totally" to be, in order to be accepting. Each of us has, to some degree, a capacity for acceptance of himself and others. The greater the capacity for acceptance, to be sure, the greater is the individual's adjustment to his life situation.

For example, in one study, children were asked to indicate on a list of twenty uncomplimentary statements, most likely true of all children, which pertained to each of them. Next each child was given a test which measured adjustment. A comparison was made of the adjustment tests and the lists of uncomplimentary statements. It was found that children who had checked the greatest number of statements had the highest adjustment scores and those who had marked the fewest statements had the lowest adjustment scores.[4]

Once one admits truths about himself which are unflattering, he is able to take the first step toward more effective behavior. Acceptance has a cumulative effect. As an acquaintance with a gift for mixing metaphors once said, "It's a hot potato that's beginning to snowball and it's only the tip of the iceberg." The expanded, more varied experience which results from acceptance leads to an expanded

[3] Abraham H. Maslow, *Motivation and Personality*, New York, Harper, 1954, pp. 388-389.
[4] Arthur W. Combs and Donald Syngg, *Individual Behavior*, New York, Harper & Brothers, 1959, pp. 244-245.

self-concept. That, in turn, decreases the need to deny or distort experiences, thus leading to increased adequacy. The more adequate one feels, the more accepting he becomes.

As parents, then, we ought to strive both in our response style and in our feeling style, to demonstrate acceptance of our children and to help them become more accepting of themselves—more adequate.

In Chapter Ten we discussed major kinds of responses to communication: advice-giving, probing, supportive, interpretive and paraphrasing. The effect of each of these response styles on communication was examined in terms of parenting. The superiority of the paraphrasing response was indicated.

Next we spoke about the different kinds of feeling style: the nice guy, the achiever, the logical thinker and the authentic person. These too were examined in light of how they influence parental roles and affect communication and the psychological growth process.

The chapter concluded with a comment on the need for increasing one's acceptance of himself and others. In particular, as a parent you need to help your child become more self-accepting. It's the first step along the road to the kind of effective behavior you desire and, indeed, that your child desires.

In Chapter Eleven we're going to find out more about response style. Specifically, we'll deal with the paraphrase and how to develop the ability to respond to feelings so that, by example, you will be able to teach your child how to listen.

Chapter 11

Once more, but this time with feeling.

As I began to write this chapter, I was reminded of the
story of the little boy who wouldn't get off the toy horse.
It happened just before Christmas one year in Wana-
maker's department store in New York City.

A young mother was doing her annual present-buying
in the store. Her little boy—age about five—had discovered
a life-like stuffed horse in the toy department and had
climbed up on it. No amount of pleading on mother's part
could persuade him to get out of the saddle. She pretend-
ed departure from the store by hiding behind a column.
Even that didn't faze the young cowboy who was "gid-
dyapping" gleefully and boisterously trying to "break" the
bucking bronco.

Seeing her plight, the manager approached her and
asked if he could be of some help. Could he get her son
off the horse, she wondered. He said he would try.

Rather than going to the youngster, the manager went
to where Santa Claus was seated and spoke to him. Santa
nodded his understanding of the problem and said he
would use a bit of psychology. He walked to the child,
bent over so that his mouth was against the boy's ear and
whispered something.

Immediately the lad jumped down off the horse and ran
straight for his mother, eyes wide. As the pair moved

down the aisle, the manager asked Santa what he had said that got such quick results.

"I told him that Santa wanted him to get off the horse and go with his mother, and that if he didn't get off the horse at once, Santa would break his little fingers one by one."

That's a terrible story, I know. Nevertheless, even such a bad example contains something worth emulating. Santa was precise in what he wanted the boy to do and as extreme as it is, he was equally precise in stating what the consequences of non-compliance would be. Most of the young parents I have seen, although much more humane, are not that precise. I am astounded at the number of them who seem to feel a need to get their child's permission when they give a direction:

"It's time to come in now, O.K.?" Or,

"Let's get your room cleaned up now, O.K.?"

I haven't mentioned it, but it needs mentioning and that story presents the opportunity: *Be positive! Be firm!*

Don't say, "Let's get ready for bed, now, O.K.?" Instead say:

"Please get ready for bed now."

"Please get your room cleaned up now." (You can be polite and still be firm and positive.)

Now let's proceed. I want to give you another alternative to the "I'll break your little fingers one at a time" approach to getting your child to listen.

When you bought this book, you were intrigued by the idea that it would contain some "tricks" which would help you talk to your child. Moreover, you expected to learn how to put your words into a form which would cause your child to do what you want him to do.

I believe that you have been taught some tricks of communication. I know that if you follow the suggestions in even one of the foregoing chapters, your life with your family will be more full and satisfying.

I'm also convinced that if you will follow the teachings contained in this book, you will be able to get your child to do what you want him to do. More importantly, he will do what you want not merely because *you* want him to, but because *he* wants to. The reason is that what you want him to do, in essence, is to behave in a more effective manner. He wants that too.

Behaving effectively has an ultimate payoff for your child. Within the specific limits you set, it gets him what he wants. It has an ultimate payoff for you too, because when your child behaves effectively, he also behaves acceptably. It can't be stated often enough: your child truly wants to please you. If that doesn't happen, it's because he doesn't know how.

Given a situation in which he can choose alternatives, one of which pleases you and is acceptable, the other displeasing and unacceptable, he may choose the latter. If he does, it's because your efforts to communicate the alternatives and their consequences are short-circuited or because you made it more attractive for him to do so.

We have already seen how improper reinforcement of behavior produces unfortunate results. You know that reinforcing unacceptable behavior—even when you think you're punishing it—merely produces more of that behavior. Now let's take a final and summary look at the give-and-take of parent-child communication. We're going to begin with you, the parent, and show you how to listen to what your child is really saying; not just with your ears, but totally.

The word is "empathy." It comes from the Greek words, "en," meaning in, and "pathos," which means suffering. Webster defines empathy as "Imaginative projection of one's own consciousness into another being."[1] The definition falls far short of the full meaning of the word.

In actual practice, empathy is a difficult thing for most of us. Although some few do seem naturally to possess the ability to be empathic, it is actually a skill which they developed. The knack can be acquired with practice. When you worked on paraphrase in Chapter Ten, you made a beginning, because paraphrase includes empathy as its highest refinement.

In this chapter we're going to work on the art of identi-

---

[1] Webster's Collegiate Dictionary, Fifth Edition, Springfield, Massachusetts, G. & C. Merriam Co., 1947.

fying with the feelings which underlie your child's messages. That's what empathy is all about: first you ask yourself, "What does my child *really* mean? What do his words and his body language *really* convey? How does he feel right now?" Then you convey to him what you perceive his feelings to be at that moment. When you employ empathy, it's easy to get your child to listen.

As we learned in the early chapters of this book, most of us tend to keep our feelings bottled up within us because we have never learned how to let them out, and because no one has ever tried to help us get them out. As you become more skilled at paraphrasing with empathy, you will be able to help your child identify his feelings and describe them. The end result will be deeper understanding of one another.

As your child becomes more attuned to himself as a feeling person, he will be able to deal with his feelings more effectively. With feelings under control, the kinds of knee-jerk behaviors which are unacceptable become fewer. He can make decisions which are based on rational consideration of ultimate consequenecs. As he comes to see you as someone who cares about how he feels, he will, in turn, care about how you feel.

Admonitions to children are most likely to fall on deaf ears when they are motivated by parental selfishness. Empathic based direction works because it is centered in the child, not in the parent.

Now that I've given a "sales pitch" on behalf of empathy, let's get to work. Most of this chapter is going to consist of examples of how to use the empathic response. In Chapter Ten I showed you how to paraphrase. For the most part, we limited ourselves to low-level paraphrases, those which reflect only the content or words of the message. I did provide a hint of paraphrase which reflects not only the content, but also a bit of the feeling behind the words. Let's review for a moment.

If your child comes home and says, "Mr. Smith gave us three chapters to read in the geography book. And we have to outline them, too! By Monday!", you paraphrase thus:

"You say that you have three chapters to read and out-line by Monday?"

That's a paraphrase of content, as you recall. You restate the content of the message. Since your restatement was correct, you probably will not get a reply or at the most, simply, "Yeah," and the conversation will be over.

On the other hand, suppose the dialogue goes some-thing like this:

"Dad, I called you at the office to let you know where I was going this afternoon after school. I tried at least four times but I couldn't get through."

"You mean when you called the phone didn't ring?"

That paraphrase—a probing response—will more than likely provoke a reply because it makes an unwarranted assumption.

"No, that's not what I said, Dad. I couldn't get through because every time I called I got a busy signal. You must have been on the line for at least a couple of hours."

Now junior has made an unwarranted assumption and he will get a correcting response from his father.

"No, I wasn't on the phone at all this afternoon. I was busy with reports I have to get finished by tomorrow."

It doesn't take much imagination to see that this conver-sation is going nowhere, except straight toward trouble. Before long, after a couple more of these exchanges, Dad is going to say,

"I don't believe you called at all. That business about the busy signal is just an excuse for not doing as you promised you would!"

Or maybe junior will blow the whole thing:

"You act as though I'm lying! Why don't you check? I'll bet you'll find your phone is out of order."

Straight paraphrase, then, generally produces one of two things: a mutual loss of interest in the subject or a dispute. Neither party to the exchange gains any increased understanding of himself or of the other.

But suppose that your response is a paraphrase that in-cludes a reflection of feeling? Let's see what might hap-pen. We'll take one statement and compare paraphrase of content with paraphrase of content *and* feeling.

"Mommy, the new boy next door pushed me and I fell down and got my new dress all dirty and I scraped my knee. I'll never play with him again!"

"First of all, stop crying! Then go and take off your dress so that I can wash it. You shouldn't have been wearing it to play, anyway. Besides, that boy is too rough. You shouldn't be playing with him."

Still crying, the child heads for the bedroom to change her clothes.

"All you care about is my dress!"

Obviously mother and daughter are not brought any closer together by mother's handling of the situation. Her response is limited to her child's words and appearance. Feelings have been ignored. Now let's try the same scene again.

"Mommy, the new boy next door pushed me and I fell down and got my new dress all dirty and I scraped my knee. I'll never play with him again!"

"Let's take care of that knee, first. Your dress can be washed. I'm sorry that you had an argument with Robert."

At least with this response, mother has acknowledged her daughter's feelings, at a very shallow or surface level, even though the response didn't *reflect* the feelings.

The child has a physical hurt. Mother has given that top priority. She has also shared her daughter's unhappiness at having a falling out with her new playmate. In the future, because mother's reaction has encouraged her to do so, the child will go to her mother when she has strong feelings about something.

But, as I pointed out, that exchange represents only an unspoken acknowledgement of surface feelings. Let's go a bit deeper, using the same example.

"Mommy, the new boy next door pushed me and I fell down and got my new dress all dirty and I scraped my knee. I'll never play with him again!"

"Oh, dear! You did scrape your knee badly. It must really hurt. Let's put something on it to take the pain away. I'm sure you must feel badly that Robert pushed you."

In this instance, mother not only acknowledges the physical injury, but labels her understanding of how her daughter feels. The response reflects not only the feeling of hurt which accompanies the scraped knee, but also the feeling which goes with being psychologically hurt because her playmate pushed her.

Even at this level of empathic paraphrase, mother might evoke a reply from her child which is at a deeper level of understanding of feelings. The child might reply, for example,

"Yes, my knee does hurt . . . A little, anyway. I don't know why Robert pushed me. I thought he was my friend."

That statement indicates that the child understands that the real hurt she has experienced comes from being injured by someone she considered a friend. But most children would need a bit more help before they could make that connection. Let's see what happens when mother digs a little deeper still into the feelings which are behind her child's statement and reflects them.

"Mommy, the new boy next door pushed me and I fell down and got my new dress all dirty and I scraped my knee. I'll never play with him again!"

"Oh, dear! You did scrape your knee. It must hurt, and it's a little frightening to have something like that happen. We'll put something on it to take the pain away. And you're worried about your new dress. It isn't torn. We'll just wash it and it will be good as new. You really feel badly that Robert pushed you because you like him and you thought he was your friend. But a friend shouldn't do that and you're puzzled and angry."

If we analyze that response, it's truly empathic, because we can see that it reflects all of the content and all of the feeling (as sure as we can be about that) behind the words: The fright that goes with a physical injury; the concern about ruining a new dress and perhaps being scolded for it; the disappointment over a friendship suddenly and inexplicably gone awry; and the bewilderment and resentment occasioned by the child's experience. Mother's sensitivity to her daughter's feelings are sure to open the door to the child's greater understanding of her own feelings and how they affect her.

Let's work through another example, one that's more simple than that one, so that you get a clearer picture of the difference between the various levels of paraphrase. Here's a statement:

"I'm sixteen and I think you're being unfair! Why can't I date during the week like my friends can? Boys don't even ask me anymore."

Here's what we will term a *First Level* response. It's a paraphrase, but ignores feelings:

"Did you say that your friends are allowed to date during the week?"

A *Second Level* response would go something like this:

"You seem to feel that sixteen is grown up."

The feeling reflection may be accurate, but it's stated in such a way that it's argumentative. It also ignores some other feelings implied in the statement.

A *Third Level* response gets at the feelings in a non-argumentative manner, but only scrapes the surface:

"It sounds as though you feel frustrated because you can't do some of the things your friends can at sixteen."

The *Fourth Level* is the level of empathy. Empathic responses, remember, get beneath the surface and enlarge upon the feelings expressed and/or described.

"It seems that you're frustrated because we don't permit you to go out during the week. You're humiliated when you have to tell boys why you can't accept their invitations. You're sixteen now, and you feel that you're responsible enough to date and still get your school work done. You're afraid that you will become unpopular."

Although not one "feeling" word was included in the young lady's statement, the response contains five: frustrated, humiliated, responsible, afraid and unpopular. All are implied in the girl's claim that her parents are "unfair" and in the emphatic way she used the word. As a result of the empathic response, she will be able to understand her feeling much more fully. And her parents' understanding will permit a discussion and a mutually agreed-upon arrangement with regard to the dating.

Here's another example:

"School is a drag. If I could, I'd quit, get a job and make some money so I could leave home."

Level One response:

"Yeah, I know what you mean."

Level Two response:

"Sounds like you feel you'd enjoy work more than going to school."

Level Three response:

"You're bored with school."

Fourth Level or empathic response:

"School really turns you off because you can't see where it's going to get you. Right now a job is more attractive because money would make you independent. You feel trapped and restricted by the rules you have to follow at home."

Obviously it isn't easy to come up with empathic responses, especially when your child's statements are irritating. You can see now why it's so important for you to be able to identify your own feelings. In order for your communications with your child to produce greater harmony and understanding between you, you must remain objective and keep your feelings from getting in the way.

If your child says, "You won't let me watch TV because you don't love me anymore!" it's not easy to restrain yourself from replying:

"That's a dumb thing to say. Go to your room!"

Or to the statement, "I don't want to do my stupid homework now! I want to go out and ride my bike. I'll do my homework after dinner!" you find yourself wanting to say,

"Don't tell me what you're going to do. Now you just get busy with that homework this instant. And make sure you do it correctly!"

Anger which you believe is displayed toward you and without any reason that you are able to perceive generally causes you to become angry in turn. It's a vicious circle and unfortunately, at each turn the anger becomes more intense until communication is closed off.

The reason this happens is that the anger is poured into

sarcastic and biting dialogue and never really brought out into the open. If you're angry, say so, and get it out of the way:

"I'm furious."

"I am very angry because of what you did."

"I'm annoyed by your behavior."

Now let's see how the empathic response can be used to get your child to listen. You'll recognize some of the techniques we talked about in earlier chapters. First, let's set the scene.

You're in a department store with your ten year old in tow. As you pass by the toy section, he suddenly disappears. Then above the steady hum of shopping sounds, you hear his voice.

"Mom! Mom, c'mere!"

Noticing that he has managed to catch the attention of everybody in sight, you try to glide unobtrusively toward the other end of the store, but he will have none of that.

"Mom! C'mere and look at this!"

You decide to give in and you join him at the toy counter.

"Do you have to yell like that? I wish I could pretend I don't know you when you do that!"

"But mom, look at this neat ray gun. It's just like the one in the movie we saw last week. Can I have one?"

"I don't know where you get the idea that I'm made of money! What am I supposed to use to pay for it? No, you can't have one. Not unless you can buy it yourself. You do get an allowance, don't you?"

"Yeah, but I don't have enough. The ray gun costs $9.95 and all I have is seven dollars. If you buy it for me, I'll pay you back. Honest!"

"The answer is no, young man, now let's go. I have some more things I have to get."

"Aw nuts! You're mean and . . . and, you're stingy, too. I hate you!"

The lad's last words bring your anger to a boil, and earn him a slap. The focus of all eyes, you exit ungraciously, dragging your screaming offspring by his arm.

It isn't hard to realize that this was an encounter of the

worst kind. Everybody lost. Let's play the same scene, only this time with empathy.

"Mom! Mom, c'mere!"

This is the first critical point. You have two choices: ignore the call, or respond to it. Perhaps you should go your way, you think. If your child gets lost, it will teach him a lesson. But you decide to respond. There's no way you can control your child from across the store by shouting at him. Your proximity to him does give you the ability to control or at least it gives you the possibility. We'll assume that you know that and so you join your son in the toy department.

"It makes me angry when you do that. I want you to stay with me. I'm worried that you'll get lost. It's a long way home, you know." (Note how mother describes her feelings, and has them under control.)

"I'm sorry, mom, I'll stay with you from now on, but look at this ray gun! It's just like the one in the movie we saw last week. Can I have one?"

"If you have enough money to pay for it. I still have some shopping to do. I can't spare $9.95 plus tax."

"I don't need that much, mom, I have my allowance money that I saved. See, (pulling a wad of bills and change from his pocket) I have more than seven dollars. All I need is three more. You can spare that much can't you? Please, mom?"

"Yes, I can spare three dollars. And I can see you're excited and eager to have the ray gun but if you really want it you're going to have to earn the three dollars. Or you can pay me back out of your allowance. If you want to earn the money, I've got some chores you can do. Which is it going to be? Earn the money, or pay it back from your allowance?" (Mother provides a controlled choice.)

"I'd like to get my allowance and save some of it. I'll do the chores and earn the money. What do I have to do?"

But what if you can't spare the three dollars? Or what if your son didn't save any of his allowance and needs the entire ten dollars?

If you don't have an allowance system for your child, I'd strongly recommend that you consider initiating one.

It's an excellent way to teach a child how to handle money.

Allowances should have no strings attached. That is, they should not be conditional on doing chores or on good behavior or the like. An allowance should be considered the child's share of the family income. He can earn additional money by doing chores if you choose to arrange that with him.

Like your income, allowances should be large enough to cover fixed expenses. Out of his allowance your child should be expected to pay for his school lunch, bus fare, club dues and those kinds of things. The amount should be enough so that, just as you can, with good management, your child can put a little aside in savings.

There isn't any standard amount which you should give as an allowance. It depends on your own income.

Forgive that digression, but the matter of allowance frequently comes up when I talk with parents and there's much confusion about it. It seemed appropriate at this point to cover the subject briefly. Now let's get back to the question of what to do if you can't spare the money for the ray gun. Here's the way it might be handled:

"See, I have more than seven dollars. All I need is three more. You can spare that, can't you? Please, mom?"

"No, I'm sorry, but I really can't spare three dollars. I have one more item I just have to get, and it will use up all of my money."

"Aw, c'mon, mom, please can I get the ray gun?"

"I know you really want that toy and I know you're disappointed that you can't have it today, but I can't give you the money. I'll tell you what I'll do. I have to come downtown again next Monday to go to the dentist. If you still want the ray gun, I'll lend you the money and I'll come in and get it for you then. That's the best I can do."

There's no bargaining in that offer. It's a take it or leave it proposition, and yet, nobody loses. Let's look at the entire episode again, from the beginning.

The first thing mother did was to get in touch with her own feelings when junior separated from her and went off on his own to the toy department. She was angry and worried. She shared those feelings with her son.

In the first case, where she did have the money, she reflected her son's feelings of excitement and eagerness. But she didn't just hand over the money. She made a learning experience out of the situation. She not only taught him that "there's no such thing as a free lunch," but also permitted him to share in the decision-making process: pay back the three dollars out of his allowance or earn it by doing some chores.

In the second case, not having the money, she reflected her son's disappointment and then presented a solution to the problem. She prevented a scene, because there was no room for argument in her offer.

Let's take another situation. Pretend that you come home unexpectedly and discover your fifteen-year-old daughter, Laurel, in bed with a young man. How would you react? Considering the difficulty we have in dealing with a feeling as strong as love, it's no wonder we really mess things up when we're faced with the feelings and emotions which are known as passion and sexuality.

The usual scene would go something like this:

"This is absolutely disgusting! To do that kind of thing at all is bad enough, but to show your contempt for your father and mother by bringing this boy home! You get out of that bed this instant and put on your clothes! And you, young man, get dressed and leave before I call the police and have you arrested for rape!"

As nearly as I can recall her words, that was the way one mother who came to me for counseling had reacted when she discovered her high school sophomore daughter and a boy engaging in a sex act. I do remember that she added the word, "perverts" to her comments to the pair.

The next day her daughter and the boy were missing from school. They were located in a motel in Los Angeles—four hundred miles away. They had been traced through, of all things, a taxicab which they had stolen.

That's the recommended way for parents to deal with that sort of situation if they want to shut off completely all meaningful communication with their daughter. It is also nearly guaranteed to drive her back into the arms of the boy in another bedroom somewhere. There must be a better way. Let's try it once more, this time with feeling.

Of course you would have no choice but to make your presence known to the young lovers and take it from there. Compassion should prompt you to let them know you're in the house by slamming the door so that they don't know they have been found flagrante delicto. But if you want to confront them in the act, you might say,

"I'm as sorry as you are that I have found you like this, but I have. I am infuriated that this has happened, and especially resentful that you would do it here. I want both of you to get dressed. I'll discuss this with you downstairs, Laurel. And I want you out of this house as soon as you are dressed, young man!" With that you turn and leave the room.

That was much better. You let your daughter and the young man know precisely how you feel without shouting and without making them feel that communication is closed. But what about the follow-up? What would you say to your daughter when she joins you downstairs as you directed her to? You could let her have it with both barrels.

"I never thought I would have a cheap trollop for a daughter. How could you do this to me, after all I've done for you? Is this what you do to show your gratitude? The next thing you'll do to drive me to an early grave is tell me you're pregnant. What did I ever do to deserve this?"

Let's try it with empathy:

"I wouldn't be honest, Laurel, if I didn't tell you that I am shocked. I'm so disappointed to find that you took advantage of my absence. I feel betrayed."

"I'm so sorry, mother."

"Yes, I'm sure you are. And you should be. You should be sorry. But not for me, for yourself. Not just for the fact that I found you having sex—there's much more for you to be regretful about, Laurel."

"I don't know what you mean. I won't get pregnant, if that's what you mean. I've been taking the pill for a couple of months now . . ."

"Yes, I was worried about pregnancy and I'm relieved that you had the good sense to protect yourself. But that's not what I mean. You must realize that there's more for you to be concerned about. Look, Laurel, I'm not going to moralize and tell you that sex is wrong when you're not married. If you haven't learned how we feel about that by now, your father and I have missed the boat completely. And I know that under the proper conditions, sex is a highly enjoyable activity. I know also that it seems to be the most popular topic. Radio, movies, TV, newspapers are filled with it. The temptation to try it must be enormous for young people . . ."

"I wouldn't have sex with just any boy, mother. I love Brad, and he loves me. I've never done it with anybody else. It just happened. We didn't plan it."

"Laurel, how old is Brad?"

"Sixteen."

"And you love him a great deal."

"Yes."

"Do you plan to get married?"

"Well, not now—I mean Brad has to finish school first, and he wants to be a lawyer. It's so hard to wait that long to be together . . ."

I think you can see the advantage of this way of dealing with the situation between Laurel and her mother. The avenue of communication is kept open. Mother hasn't estranged her daughter and she didn't close the door of their home to the young man forever, either. That would have forced Laurel into a very difficult and unnecessary choice, one that could be tragic.

Laurel has to see for herself the impossibility of the situation. It would be useless—and damaging to their relationship—for her mother to preach. Marriage is out, a living-together arrangement is also out of the question. She must also see the effect her actions will have on her parents and their feelings if she continues to bed down with Brad, and she must appreciate the effect on her friends. Even if they accept her liaison with Brad, it will soon become common knowledge and their parents are not likely to permit their socializing with Laurel and Brad.

The point is, Laurel's mother has approached a bad situation in such a way that she can make the best of it. She and Laurel can still talk, and best of all, Laurel will be willing to listen. She hasn't told Laurel what to do but she has set the stage so that she can explore the alternatives and the consequences with her.

Let's set the scene for another problem. We'll work this one through together, and you can try your wings.

You have called your daughter—a fifth grader—three times and still have had no response. You go to the door of her room.

"Becky, if you don't get up right now and get ready for breakfast, you're going to be late for school!"

"I'm not going to school. I hate school and I hate Mrs. Blake!"

Your normal reaction, if you're typical, would be something such as:

"Of course you're going to school. You know you like school *and* Mrs. Blake. You *have* to go to school. And besides, it isn't nice to say you hate anyone."

That's a straight reaction to the content. And note how it denies the child the right to describe what she believes is her feeling at the moment. What will happen next? I'd wager it would go like this:

"No, I'm not going! (At this point the tears will start.) And I do hate Mrs. Blake. I hate her. She's mean!"

It's pretty clear that nobody can win this one. It can only get worse from here on, so let's run it back and try "listening to heartbeats," as a magazine editor once titled an article I had written on the subject of empathy.

What I'd like you to do is write an empathic response and then write the dialogue the way you think it would ensue. Don't look at my suggestion until you're finished.

"Becky, if you don't get up right now and get ready for breakfast, you're going to be late for school!"

"I'm not going to school. I hate school, and I hate Mrs. Blake!"

Because you are now an empathic person, you're going to ignore the content momentarily and reach for the feeling. Reacting to what's behind the words, you say,

"It sounds as though something happened at school that has really upset you. You're worried about going to school. I'd like to listen if you want to talk about it."

Maybe it isn't worry that your daughter is feeling, but if you don't hit the feeling precisely, that's all right. You have let her know that you care about how she feels, and if you didn't "read" her correctly, she'll let you know:

"I'm mad at Mrs. Blake. She yelled at me in front of the whole class. She said I didn't do my homework, and I did!"

So it isn't worry after all, it's anger and embarrassment. Respond to those feelings.

"You're angry with Mrs. Blake because she scolded you. You were embarrassed and you feel she was unfair." (Children are very concerned about being treated fairly.)

"Yeah! And all the kids laughed at me."

Angry, embarrassed, and a bit resentful. Mainly, it's the embarrassment that makes Becky want to stay home, it appears.

"It made you feel badly when you were laughed at."

"Yeah, I felt so dumb."

"What do you think you should do?"

"I'd like to show her that I did do my homework. It's right here in my book. I didn't hear her when she told us to turn in the papers."

"That's a good thing to do. Are you going to mail it to her?"

"Of course not! I want to give it to her and tell her I had it all the time. Then she'll feel sorry she yelled at me."

"Well, then, hadn't you better get up?"

Now wasn't that a much more pleasant way to deal with the problem? Everybody will eventually come out winners.

Don't say it won't work. It will. How did we match up?

There are a couple of points about this method of stimulating conversation on the feeling level that I want to leave you with. First of all, you must respect your child's right to privacy. By that I mean the sharing of feelings has to be a voluntary thing. Let me give you an example.

"Aren't you going outside to play this afternoon, dear?"

"Nope."

"Your friends are outside..."

"They're not my friends! They don't like me."

"Sounds like they did something that has you down-in-the-dumps."

"Yup."

"Want to talk about it?"

"Nope."

What do you do now? Well, what you have to do is respect your child's right to remain silent. After all, even suspected criminals have that right. But you do get in the last word:

"All right, dear, but if you want to talk about it later, I'll be ready to listen."

Experience will teach you, if it hasn't already, that squabbles among children tend to settle themselves. When my own children were growing up, I had many opportunities to see how things get fouled up when parents get the notion that they must play Henry Kissinger, or worse still, take sides. The day following a seemingly insoluble dispute, the children are playing together as though nothing had happened. But their parents may never again be on speaking terms.

So the thing to remember is that once you have reflected what you believe or perceive to be your child's feelings, don't push the matter if he doesn't wish to. Just let him know that you're ready to lend an ear at any time in the future he might wish to pursue the issue.

The second point about using empathic responses, like the first, is also a word of caution. Don't over-use it.

There are times when one of the responses—interpretation, probing, advice-giving and supporting are preferable to the empathic response. I can't tell you when those times are. With practice, you will become aware enough of the psychological needs of your children to be able to make that judgment yourself.

As you become used to responding to feelings, you'll also learn to watch the effect your response has on your child. It's that skill which will enable you to get your child to listen.

In Chapter Eleven we concentrated on responding to your child's feelings with empathic paraphrase. Underlying the ability to respond with empathy are a lot of the techniques which you learned in earlier chapters. No matter which of the particular sub-skills we discussed seem to appeal to you, or even if you prefer to ignore all of them and "wing it" yourself, please remember this: whatever means you use to control your child, please consider his feelings in the process. Empathy may be the greatest bargain you will ever find to help with your parenting. It doesn't cost a cent, and it pays off better than a daily double.

Chapter Twelve represents graduation. It's the final chapter. When you finish it, you will know all you really need to know about working effectively with children. What we're going to talk about in the ensuing pages is how you can get a teenager to listen. Yes, it can be done if you know a little bit about the adolescent psyche.

Chapter 12

How to get your teenager to listen.

IN this chapter we're going to be talking about the child who is somewhere between thirteen and fifteen years of age. I'll refer to this period as either the "teens" or "preadolescence." Whatever the term used, this is a turbulent stage of development. If you and your child get through it successfully, there should be smoother waters ahead.

The focus of our attention will be on communication. We'll try to help you avoid the kinds of problems parents so frequently encounter when they try to communicate with their teenaged children.

The time frame which will be our major concern in these pages is generally acknowledged to be the most difficult—for both child and parents. It's a period when the transition is made from an almost totally child-centered environment to one which has gradually widened so that experiences are socially centered. One example is the abrupt change in the educational program.

The child is usually in the seventh, eighth or ninth grade. In most school systems, his program is no longer confined to one "self-contained" class. He must move from classroom to classroom and do so in a brief "passing" period.

Where previously he had only one teacher all day, with whom he could share confidences and otherwise identify, now there are several. His daily social contacts when he reaches seventh grade are suddenly expanded to include not thirty children, but hundreds.

Each of his teachers sees not thirty children, but as many as two hundred or more each day. Of necessity, the teachers' emphasis is no longer on the individual child, but on the subject taught. One need only follow a group of incoming seventh graders around school on their first day to be able to appreciate the bewilderment they experience.

As hard to accept as it may be, teenagers no longer are children. True, they're only a little bit older and only a little bit wiser. Even though some of the things they do would tend to refute the latter difference, nevertheless, there *is* a difference between childhood and preadolescence that goes beyond the physical changes. That small difference, if not understood—and respected—makes communication between parent and teenager nearly impossible.

It was pointed out earlier that parents must face the fact that one can't *make* a child do anything he doesn't want to, and that includes listen. That goes double for teenagers. When parents tell me, "That child has a mind of his own," I don't think that they really know how accurate those words are. In this chapter we're going to explore that phenomenon. I believe you'll gain a better understanding of your teenager's view of his world and why it so often seems that he lives alone in your home.

Although it may appear so, your child didn't (or won't) become a teenager overnight. The reason it seems that way is because of the way growth takes place.

Somewhere between the ages of nine and thirteen (usually about a year to two years sooner for girls), your child reaches a resting period in his physiological development. There is a sudden dip in rate of growth. This is called the preadolescent stage.

Following this preadolescent drop in the velocity of development, there is a sudden and rapid resumption of growth; first in height, and then in weight. The secondary sex characteristics make their appearance. Girls fill out and develop breasts and hips; boys go through the embarrassing change of voice and also develop bigger muscles. These changes occur over a period of about five to six years, although this varies greatly with each individual child.

Because all this acceleration in growth requires greater amounts of fuel, the preadolescent often makes his parents wish they could put a lock on the door of the refrigerator. The quantity of food consumed has no correlation to recommended daily amounts of vitamins and minerals or the basic food groups. Coca Cola at eight in the morning and junk food at any time typify food preferences.

Because growth is uneven, like the puppy that will have to go some to grow in proportion to his feet, the preadolescent tends to be clumsy. He is also restless and his parents and teachers often see him as being lazy, rebellious, uncooperative and hypercritical.

The preadolescent boy is intensely loyal to his friends and they form a social group which is very close-knit. Girls too tend to form such groups, but the loyalty is not quite so strong. For both boys and girls at this stage, belonging to the peer group and being accepted by its members is a prime need.

Interests center in a variety of activities. Team sports, TV, radio (music), movies, all occupy much of the preadolescent's time. Although currently changes are taking place in the teen society in terms of sex roles, there are still great differences between the interests of girls and boys.

Other needs of the preadolescent are information about and understanding of the physiological changes that are, or will be, taking place. Parents and other adults with whom they come in contact must be warm and understanding—difficult as that may be at times.

The day before I sat down to write this chapter I attended a meeting of school personnel. Seated at my right was an assistant superintendent. At one point in the discussion of the school program, he turned to me and said,

"I think there ought to be a law against seventh and eighth graders."

Of course that superintendent was joking (at least I believe he was joking), but his remark does point up the difficulty adults have in dealing with the preadolescent. It really doesn't have to be that hard, provided that up to the beginning of preadolescence you have played your parental cards correctly.

Several times during the preceding chapters of this book I suggested that during the very early years, parents ought to begin preparing their children for independence. Moreover, they should begin early to prepare *themselves* for the time when their children want to become independent.

At the beginning of this chapter it was stated that there is a small, but significant difference between childhood and preadolescence. I said that unless parents understand and respect that difference, their attempts to communicate with their teenage children will be difficult, if not impossible. Let's take a close look at this difference.

When your child is (or was) small, your relationship with him was that of giver and taker. You supplied the means of subsistence—food, shelter, physical care—and his psychological needs. Along with that and because of it, there was the unspoken relationship between you which said that you were the superior person. "Mother knows best," "Trust your father, he knows what's good for you," are expressions which characterize the respective roles. In this relationship, your child at first was completely willing to accede to all your directions. And all of your messages to him carried the additional message that you were in the superior position.

If you managed your parenting well, gradually the complementary nature of the parent-child relationship changed. Little by little, your child was permitted to make decisions about his life. You still guided the choices and you still saw to it that he did not choose dangerous alternatives, but still he was allowed to make decisions.

Over a period of years the learning process widened. An increasing number of decisions was permitted. With your guidance, your child has grown in his feeling of confidence with regard to his decisions and his decisions increased in quality. Parallel with that growth there has been a gradual change in your relationship too.

The giver-taker relationship slowly became something different. Yes, you still provided the food, clothing and shelter, and yes, your child still needed the psychological support. But instead of unquestioned acceptance of the notion of mother and father knowing what's best in all things, and being the superiors, your child has developed a new need. He has begun to want a greater control over his life.

The point at which the need for this kind of control really comes to the surface is during the preadolescent period. It's the difference between childhood and preadolescence which I spoke of earlier. It's what causes the greatest amount of parent-teen communication failures: the need for independence.

All of a sudden, it seems, your child no longer is willing to accept the inferior position in your relationship. Instead he wants a relationship which is characterized by equality. It isn't enough now to say, "Do this because I said so," or because "We know what's best for you," now your orders come under examination and questioning. Those which run counter to what your child desires or has decided, you can bet he will dispute.

What you have to say—your wishes with regard to the way he conducts his affairs—runs a poor second to what "the gang" thinks, in the event you have conflicting views. So if you try to get through this period by conducting a tug-of-war with your child's peer group, with him as the rope, everyone loses. The question is, how can you handle things so that everyone wins?

First of all, of course, you must recognize and respect your child's desire and need to be independent. That's awfully difficult if you have not provided the kinds of experiences during the early years which must precede independence. In that event neither you nor your child will have confidence in his ability to handle his independence. But don't despair if that's your present circumstance. It isn't too late to provide training for independent decision-making even during the preadolescent years. Preadolescents still require guidance.

It will continue to be necessary for you to meet your

teenagers need for independence by letting him make decisions, but you will have to provide a greater measure of encouragement and guidance as he does so, just as you would with a much younger child. And as with smaller children, preadolescents who have not had practice in decision-making will make "bad" decisions. If those bad decisions can result in consequences which will be harmful, you will have to try to prevent them.

Fortunately, with smaller children, you can prevent decisions from being made which have the potential for psychological or physical damage. With a preadolescent, short of locking him up, all you can do is *attempt* to prevent harmful decisions.

Let's assume that you did train your child in decision-making. Because you did provide that kind of training, your child is able to handle a large measure of independence. Further, because you began early to relinquish the reins, you are not suddenly faced with a child who demands that you allow him to let go of your apron strings. You have been preparing for this throughout your child's developing years. Now that the time is here, letting go is not a traumatic event.

Unfortunately, though, many parents don't do enough to prepare themselves or their children for independence. Then, when it's demanded, it's begrudgingly and fearfully granted and poorly used.

Under those conditions, parents attempt to maintain the superiority-inferiority relationship to the greatest extent possible. This causes frequent or continual conflict. Given the diversity of influences outside the home, efforts to do your teenager's thinking for him, or to direct his behavior, are not only exhausting, they're impossible.

As hard as parents may try to show their "muscle" in their relationship with their teenaged child, the efforts simply are destined not to be effective. The reason is that, at the same time, their child is doing things to show his equality. There's a continuing contest of "one-upmanship." To prove his point, the child will do the things he knows his parents abhor the most, just to show them he can't be manipulated or controlled by them.

Psychiatrist Rudolph Dreikurs speaks of families which are constantly "at war," partially as a result of changes in our culture which "pit children against adults."[1] In rejecting these changes, parents set up a conflict situation, one from which they will most surely emerge the losers.

What teenagers want most is power; power over their own conduct, for example. When their parents tell them not to do something, it provides a perfect opportunity for teenagers to show that they have power. They simply disregard the prohibition. So strong is the need for a sense of power that they may even tell their parents they have done the forbidden thing when in fact they haven't.

At times the rebellion is so clear-cut that it seems to be an automatic reaction. One father told me that he had decided the only way to handle his son was to insist that he refrain from doing all the things which were acceptable. The father reasoned that having been *forbidden* to do the "right" things, the boy was certain to defy his parents and do them anyway.

As odd as it may seem, there's more truth than humor in that idea. Very often your teenager will suggest that he's going to engage in some behavior or other and what he wants is for you to tell him not to. Teenagers are not beyond the need for support, for example, when their peers are urging them to engage in activities which they find are in conflict with their accustomed behavior or their beliefs.

During a counseling session, a freshman high school girl once told me that her girl friends had organized a weekend trip and wanted her to go with them. When the girl found out that the objective was to have an opportunity to sleep with the boys on the basketball team, she didn't want to go.

Rather than tell the other girls that, she agreed to accompany them, provided her parents gave their permission. Secretly, she was hoping they would refuse.

Even though she wanted them to say she couldn't go, she confided to me that when they did refuse permission,

"I found myself arguing with them, trying to convince them to let me go. At one point I even said I'd go no matter what they said. It was weird. I don't know why I did it."

As the colloquialism has it, the young lady was "caught between a rock and a hard place." On the one hand, she had her reasons for not wanting to go with her friends and on the other, she had a need to feel that if she wanted to go, she could do so in spite of her parents' wishes to the contrary.

The need for power is universal. "People Power," "Black Power," "Chicano Power," "Parent Power," and even "Kid Power," are the rallying cries of various groups. Each of these is fine, provided the power is exerted within the framework of cooperation and "democratic" processes.

A good example of the failure of power which is exerted in the context of the inferior-superior relationship is the prevalent use of marijuana. Young people use it in spite of their parents' attempts to prevent them from doing so. Adults use the drug in spite of legislation against it.

Like prostitution, the demand for marijuana proved to be more decisive than attempts to pass laws forbidding it. Finally, in both cases, the efforts were shifted from prohibition to control. We seem to have reached a point where what can't be prevented by enacting legislation, we make legal.

Parents of teenagers shouldn't accede to their children's demands in a similar manner. Simply to say, "OK, I give up, go ahead and do what you want. You have my approval," is to shortchange your child. In the first place, he may not be seeking your approval. He may really want you to say, "No, I don't want you to do that." Or he may want you to say, "Let's sit down and talk about this. Maybe there are some things I don't understand and perhaps I can point out some things you aren't aware of."

Parents don't have all the answers. We don't have all the information, either.

I recall the case of a father who returned home from a trip to discover his son had been smoking "pot." To say the least, the incident was interesting for both. The boy, caught completely off guard, took the offensive.

"Well, I guess it must come as a shock to find that someone in your own family uses a drug."

"Well, yes, a bit, but I'm more surprised than shocked, son."

"I suppose you're going to tell me to stop using it."

"No, that would cause a problem for both of us. If you want to continue smoking marijuana you'll do it. It won't matter if I forbid it. I will say that I don't want you to, though, and . . ."

"Why not? I've made a study of it, and I know it's not harmful."

"No, I don't oppose it only on that basis. I know the research hasn't really been conclusive, and I'll admit that you probably have more information on that score than I have. Still I'd rather you wouldn't smoke it until all the facts are known. But I have another reason."

"Well why, then?"

"Because it's illegal. I don't want you to break the law and I'm certainly not going to be a party to it. If you insist on smoking marijuana, I can't stop you. But please respect my wishes and don't smoke it in this house."

"OK, dad, I promise I won't."

That was a case in which the problem was resolved by agreement. It may have been preferable if the boy had said he would never again smoke marijuana—and meant it. But the father knew that he *wouldn't* really mean it, so he didn't rant and rave and try to extract such a promise.

The father also let his son know that he didn't approve of the use of marijuana. But he didn't put the young man down by intimating his decision to use marijuana was done without any consideration of possible physical damage, nor did he try to give the impression that his knowledge of the drug was superior to his son's. Finally, he made no attempt to force his son to comply. Instead, he sought cooperation.

The key to handling that kind of situation is to discuss. An exchange of ideas will get your child to listen. An argument will not. Holding to your values and refusing to concede will gain your child's respect. Giving in will not.

Remember that communications with teenagers on matters where there are strong feelings on both sides need not bear immediate fruit. Some issues between parents and teens will require extended discussion. It's no less a diplomatic mission than those which take place between nations. When you reach an impasse, it may be necessary to say, "OK, this doesn't seem to be getting us anywhere. Let's knock off for today. Maybe tomorrow we'll be able to reach an agreement."

Keep in mind these points which we've covered in Chapter Twelve: the teenager's need for independence, and his need to feel that he is not being put in a one-down position. Within those guidelines, the techniques we covered in earlier chapters are just as applicable to teenagers.

Be an objective listener. Try to keep your own feelings from interfering with the communication process. Don't let your anger get in the way of your attention to your preadolescent's feelings, for example.

Remember that the message isn't necessarily in the words your child utters. In fact, they may actually be a "smoke screen" for his real message. Become adept at reading body language. If your teenager's facial expression or gestures appear to be incongruent with what he has said, for example, you may be better off to go with them.

Timing is important in any discussion. If you want to raise the issue of your daughter's lateness in coming home from her last date, don't bring it up just before this evening's escort is to arrive to pick her up.

Tone of voice is another important clue. Words which seem to be given emotional emphasis may have some significance for your young son or daughter far beyond what the words themselves would indicate.

Be emphatic. Listen to the entire message when your teenager speaks with you. Reflect the feelings behind his words, at least as you perceive those feelings to be. Then check your perception.

Finally, make your own messages clear. And before you say what you have on your mind, make sure you have your child's attention. You might even preface your message with a statement such as, "Please give me your attention. I have something I want to say to you." That approach will help to insure that your teenager will be all ears. It worked for Marc Anthony.

There is an adage which is often quoted: "The poor workman blames his tools." In this book you have been given many tools. They have been proven. If they don't work for you, you should take a close look at the way you have applied them. To quote another adage, "If at first you don't succeed, try, try again."

I don't want to imply that the techniques presented between the covers of this book are the only ones there are, or that they are the best. In my conversations with parents and in working with parent groups, I have found that they have developed ways of dealing with problems which are very effective. If you have developed procedures which you find are working for you, please don't abandon them. Instead, see if those suggested in this book can somehow improve on them, or make them even more effective. But there are some general recommendations, and I have recapped them in the following paragraphs.

Remember the principle of reinforcement. To a child who is desperate for the attention of his parents, being punished by them can be reinforcing. Don't make the common mistake and permit your child—or your teenager—to earn that kind of bootleg payoff for unacceptable behavior.

Be positive. Look for all the commendable things your child does. Let him know that you're aware of them. That's much more effective than waiting for him to behave unacceptably and then reacting to it in a negative way.

Above all, don't preach. Communicate. Listen to what your child is saying. Let him know you have listened. That's how to get your child to listen.

Appendix A

Auditory Exercises

It's always a good idea to begin the search for causes of poor listening with a thorough examination of your child's hearing. A child who doesn't seem to respond to directions may be unable to do so because he can't hear them. If your child hasn't had a hearing examination, have that done before you try to do any of the following exercises with him.

A thorough examination includes more than just the ability to hear. Even though your child may be able to hear your voice, he may not be able to discriminate between the sounds he hears, or they may not be intelligible to him. A specialist can determine whether those sorts of problems exist.

Assuming that you have found your child's hearing to be normal, or within normal limits, there are some things you can do together which will sharpen up his listening skills. Remember these three things:

1. Make each exercise a game.
2. Don't spend too much time on any one of them or work too long at any one time. If your child has obviously lost interest, stop. Tomorrow is another day.
3. *You must be patient.* You can't force the human body to do anything it's not developmentally ready to do.

1. Fill two water glasses to different levels so that when tapped with a spoon one plays a much higher note than the other. Have your child sit with his back to you. Tap both glasses. Ask, "How many different sounds did you hear?" If he says, "One," repeat the action until he can hear two sounds. Test until you're sure he does. Next, tap

one of the glasses. Tell him to turn around and see if he can pick out the glass you tapped. Repeat this, gradually changing the water level to make the notes of the two glasses sound more alike.

2. A variation of the above exercise is to strike one of the glasses harder than the other and see if the child can identify the one that sounded louder; the one that sounded softer.

3. Have the child fill two glasses so that both play the same note when struck.

4. If you have a musical instrument available, play pairs of notes, some the same and some consisting of two different notes. Tell your child to raise his arm if the notes are different. As with the water glasses, make the notes closer together gradually, making sure your child succeeds at each step. BE CERTAIN THAT YOUR CHILD KNOWS WHAT "SAME" AND "DIFFERENT" MEAN. Many kindergarteners do not.

5. The PDQ Test for auditory discrimination consists of word pairs, some of which are the same word and some of which are different words but have similar sounds. For example, bin-pin, third-herd, box-fox. (This is much the same as exercise 3, above, but using words instead of notes.) Obviously the most direct way to train a child to learn to discriminate between the sounds of language is to use language sounds. Make up as many as you can of the kinds of word pairs in the example above. Have your child identify which pairs consist of the same words and which are made up of two different but similar sounding ones.

6. In a variety of environments (your backyard, downtown, at the ocean, airport, etc.) have your child close his eyes and identify as many different sounds as he can. Tell him to "listen really hard."

7. With a pencil, stick, or with your hands, tap out different rhythms. After each, instruct your child to tap out the same pattern. Begin with simple ones (e.g., the rhythm of "Shave and a haircut, two bits.") and tap slowly. Proceed gradually to more complex and more rapid ones in accordance with your child's ability to imitate correctly.

8. Give your child a sound which begins a word. Have him say as many words as he can which begin with the same sound. Repeat this with a number of different beginning sounds. For example; sit, so, sun, sat, sore.

9. Play a variation of Simon Says. When you give the directions your child is to mimic, make your actions disagree with your words. Your child is to ignore your actions and

do as "Simon Says." As an example, "Simon Says, 'Put your hands on your hips.'" As you say this, you put your hands on your head. Your child must put his hands on his hips. Make the directions increasingly more complex, but don't cause excessive frustration.

10. Show your child several familiar objects. As he watches, tap each in turn with a wooden spoon. Repeat two or three times slowly, asking, "Can you hear that they sound different?" When you're sure he comprehends and can hear the difference, have him face away from you. Tap each object in turn and have him identify it from its sound.

11. Place a half-dozen pictures of animals before your child. Give a description of one of the animals and have your child identify the picture of the animal you've described. Vary this with pictures of "families" of things, such as different kinds of things to sit on, different modes of transportation, different kinds of shoes, etc. Use pictures from magazines. Another variation is to have the child do the describing as you identify the picture.

12. Use your wooden spoon to tap lightly on the wall. Tap near the floor, up toward the ceiling and at the level of your child's head in random order. With his eyes closed, have your child identify the tapping as "Up high," "Down low," or "In between."

13. Tell a one sentence story: "Mary lost her hat in school." Ask, "What was lost?" "Who lost it?" "Where did she lose it?" Repeat with other such stories. Increase or decrease the difficulty and length in accordance with your child's ability.

14. Ask, "What sound does a dog make?" ". . . a cat?" ". . . a fire engine?" ". . . a motorcycle?" ". . . a vacuum cleaner?" Continue with as many different sounds as you can think of. Have your child imitate each.

15. Teach your child what rhyming words are. Present words and ask your child to say words that rhyme with them.

16. Say a sentence in which one word obviously doesn't belong. Have your child identify the word. For example, "I use a shovel when I eat," or "I heard the cat bark."

AUDITORY SEQUENTIAL MEMORY

1. Describe a series of simple actions, such as putting a book on the desk, opening a door, etc. Have your child perform the actions you have described. He must do them in the

correct order. Begin with a two-step sequence. After considerable practice a three-step sequence may be possible. A variation of this is to perform the actions and have the child describe in the correct order what you did.

2. Describe a series of actions. Have your child orally repeat the description in the same order. Again, begin with two actions and try for three.

3. Name three items in the room. Have your child go and get them or point to them and name them. Increase the number of items named in accordance with your child's ability to succeed. Four items is satisfactory for this exercise.

4. This is a variation of exercise 3. Name two objects and have your child repeat them after you in the same order. Increase the number of objects named. Once again, four is satisfactory.

5. The exercise assumes that your child has the ability to count and knows the alphabet, days and months. Begin counting and reverse the position of two of the digits. For example, say, "1,2,4,3,5,6,7, etc." Your child is to tell you which number was in the wrong place. Variations of this exercise are days and (more difficult) months and letters of the alphabet.

6. Have your child repeat a short sentence after you. Begin changing one word at a time in the sentence. For example: Say, "Here is my dog's collar." Your child is to repeat this sentence. Next say, "*This* is my dog's collar." Your child is to repeat the entire sentence with the first word changed: "This is my dog's collar." Next say, "This *was* my dog's collar." Your child is to repeat the sentence with the first two words now changed: "This was my dog's collar." Continue until the entire sentence is changed. Example: "This was your cat's toy."

7. Recite a poem or the words of a song the child is familiar with. Stop before the last word in each line. Have your child supply the missing word.

For example,

Three blind _____.
Three blind _____.
See how they _____, and so on.

Next vary the omitted word,

Three _____ mice,
_____ how they run, etc.

8. Make up sentences consisting of words familiar to your child, of increasing length. Have your child repeat them in the exact order you say them. Don't exceed your child's ability. About 6 to 10 words is satisfactory, but make the

simple words, e.g., "I walk quickly around the room and then I go to the door." Increase the length and complexity in accordance with your child's ability to perform successfully.

9. Make up a series of nonsense syllables or words that are unrelated. Say them at about one-half-second intervals. Have your child repeat the series after you in the same sequence. For example,

"Nobo nim tig har," or

"Show dog tap"

"House run heavy ball"

Increase length as appropriate.

10. Say a series of numbers and have your child repeat them in the same order, e.g., 4-2-3. Vary and increase as appropriate.

11. Say a series of numbers and have your child repeat them in reverse order, e.g. 4-2, 2-4. Vary and increase as appropriate.

12. Say a series of 3 or 4 numbers and then repeat, omitting one number. Have your child tell you the number that was omitted.

13. Teach short, simple poems or nursery rhymes. Have your child recite them for you and/or for relatives and friends. Don't force a very shy child to do the latter. Encourage, but don't insist.

14. A variation of the tapping exercise listed earlier is to tap the rhythm of familiar songs. See if your child can identify the song from the tapping of the rhythm. Have your child tap the rhythm of the song.

15. Tell a short story in which one line does not fit. Have your child try to pick out and repeat the line that is misplaced.

16. Teach games such as "Pease Porridge Hot," and "Pattacake, Pattacake, Baker Man."

17. Tell the story of the Indian Boy: "An Indian boy is going out to hunt for a bear. He goes out and slams the door. Slam the door." Have your child repeat, "Slam!" "He walks through the mud. Plop, plop, plop." He repeats the "Plop, plop, plop." "Then he walks through the grass. Swish, swish, swish." Continue the story with additional sounds. When the Indian boy sees the bear, he runs home. (Make running sounds by slapping your hands against your thighs.) As the boy hurries home, the same sounds he made going out to hunt the bear are made in reverse order. Repeat this story until your child can tell it himself, making all the sounds.

18. Have your child memorize such things as his birthday, phone number, address.

19. Tell or read a story so that only one action from it is told each day. Your child must tell you each day what has happened up to that time before you will tell him the next action. Don't expect your child to recall more than three or four actions, this is three or four days back.

20. Say, "What's missing? One o'clock, two o'clock, four o'clock," or "What day comes after Sunday?" "What number comes after four?" Vary these.

21. As your child dresses, have him say aloud what he's doing. Teach the sequence. First I do this, second I do this, etc.

22. The song, "Old MacDonald Had a Farm," is an excellent aid in developing auditory sequencing skill.

23. Another aid is a game in which more and more ideas are added. For example, say, "I went to the store." Have your child repeat this. Then say, "I went to the store to buy bread." This is repeated by the child. Then, "I went to the store to buy bread and I saw a fireman." Add ideas as appropriate to your child's ability.

24. Cut pictures of different objects from a magazine. Give the pictures to your child. Name two pictures. Your child is to put the proper pictures on the table in the sequence in which you named them. Gradually, increase to four the number of pictures you call. Vary this with blocks and different colors (use crayons), shapes, numbers and letters.

25. Before doing this exercise, teach the concept, first, middle, last or first, second, third. Put three small boxes on the table. Give your child a card with a letter on it, for example, the letter "M." Say a word with the letter "M" in it—milk. Tell your child to put the card in the first box (point to it if necessary) if the "M" was at the beginning of the word "milk," in the second (or middle box—and again, point if necessary) if the "M" is in the middle of the word "milk," etc. Give only one card with a letter on it at a time, but give words in which the letter on the card appears in different positions.

26. Place a number of familiar objects in a box. Say, "Give me the _____ and _____ from the box," naming two of the objects. Your child is to give them to you in the same sequence. Gradually increase to three or four the number of objects you ask for.

27. Teach the days of the week. Make a large calendar with the names of the days left off. Write the days on pieces of paper—enough to take care of the month—and each day

have him attach (use tape) the name of the correct day to the calendar.

28. Teach the seasons. Draw a tree on a piece of butcher paper. Make it large enough so that you can attach and remove brown (or whatever color you wish) leaves to indicate fall, and green leaves to indicate summer. Smaller leaves can be used to indicate spring, and of course no foliage at all for winter.

Appendix B

Body Image Exercises and Activities

═══════════════════════════════════

Objects in our environment don't have absolute locations. To establish the distance of an object, for example, we consider it in relationship to ourselves. Relative distances too are established on the basis of their position in relation to the position of one's own body.

While an accurate idea of the size and configuration of one's body may not be critical when considering the relative distances of the planets, accuracy is quite important in gauging how much room one needs in order to keep from bumping the sides of a doorway. Or how far the end of a diving board is from where one is standing.

To learn as efficiently as possible, children must develop an accurate body image. Without it, they cannot move efficiently through their school environment. As indicated earlier, if their image of a part of their body is inaccurate, activities involving that body part will also be inaccurate.

The exercises and activities that follow will help your child develop an accurate body image. They are useful for all children, not only those whose awkwardness might indicate that one or more skills should be developed further.

As you do these remember three things:

1. Make each exercise a game.
2. Don't spend too much time on any one of them or work too long at any one time. If your child has obviously lost interest, stop. Tomorrow is another day.
3. *You must be patient.* You can't force the human body to do anything it's not developmentally ready to do.

1. Have your child stand before a full-length mirror. Point

to and name his body parts, beginning with his head and working downward. Your child is to repeat after you.

2. Using the mirror, have your child locate his body parts. To help him learn that the body has matching halves, tell him to count his body parts. Count with him, if necessary.

3. Without the mirror, and beginning with the head, ask, "What do you have on top of your body?" Respond to correct answers by repeating them. "Yes, your head." Respond to incorrect responses by supplying the correct answer. Then have the child repeat. If he responds correctly the second time, say, "Yes, your head."

   Have him feel the shape of each body part, head, neck, shoulders, and work downward. As he feels the part, you describe it with the proper word: Feel your head. It's round," "Your neck is round in one way, but it goes straight from your head to your shoulders." "Your legs don't look like sticks. Feel. They have two sides."

4. Repeat exercise 3, but if there is a sister or brother available, have the child use him or her. You will still do the labeling and describing with him.

5. Get a piece of butcher or craft paper large enough so that your child can lie on it full length. With a felt pen or a crayon, trace around his body; head, torso, arms and legs. Have him name the body parts on his outline drawing with your help and encouragement. Next have him draw in ears, eyes, nose and mouth. Have him look in a mirror while doing this so that he comes to know the locations of these features.

6a. Have the child sit across a table from you, close enough so that you can reach out and touch. Have him put his hands under the table, with fingers extended. First touch the back of one hand with your index finger. Have him tell you which hand you touched. Label the hand for him, that is, say, "Yes, that's the hand I touched. It's your right (or left) hand." Repeat until your child can respond correctly, "You touched my right hand." Or "Right hand."

6b. Next touch a finger on one of his hands (which are beneath the table) and have him show you which one you touched. Again, name the hand the finger is on. If your child cannot do this exercise, return to 6a. Don't try to force.

7. Give your child a drawing you have prepared of a human figure which has, say, only head, torso, one arm and one leg. Using his own body as a reference, have him draw in the missing parts. A mirror is helpful, or you can have him identify parts on his own body which are not on the

drawing by feeling them, starting with his head and working downward.

8. Have your child become aware of movement sensations in each part of his body. Ask him to move each in all the directions he can. Be sure he can feel each movement, for example, have him swallow and ask where he feels it and how it feels.

9. Have your child position his body as many ways as he can. Put it in the form of an open challenge: "How many shapes can you make your body?" "Can you make it long?" "How long?" "How short can you make it?" "How straight?" "How crooked?" "How big?" "How small?" "How round?" "How flat?" and so on.

10a. Hold a pencil at a distance of about a foot and a half from the child's eyes. Ask him to focus on the eraser or the point and then move it slowly from right to left while he follows it with his eyes. His head is not to move. Hold it if necessary. Now move the pencil up and down and in a large circle. Eye movements should be smooth.

10b. A variation on this is to poke a string into a sponge rubber ball and then suspend the ball from the ceiling or the top of a doorway. Swing the ball slowly from side to side and have the child follow it with his eyes as in exercise 10a.

11. Get a hula hoop. You can make one, from a 9 foot piece of old garden hose or plastic pipe of the kind which is used for sprinkler systems, by pushing both ends of the tube into a piece of broomstick. Have your child roll it and then try to run through it without touching it as it's rolling.

12. Get a six foot length of rope and have your child place it on the ground or floor in any shape he wishes. Then tell him to "See if you can walk the rope so that your feet are always on it." Have him do this forward and then backward, upright and on hands and knees.

13. Place the rope on the ground or floor in a straight line. Say, "I want you to see if you can jump over the rope." After he jumps, say, "Good, now how many ways can you jump over the rope?" Accept and encourage all efforts. Example: one foot, forward, backward, etc.

14. Arrange an obstacle course inside or outside of the house. Be inventive and have a good variety of obstacles. The idea is to have the child get his body into as many different positions as possible.

15a. On a ten foot length of butcher or craft paper, draw circles which duplicate the positions of the child's hands and knees when crawling in a cross pattern (left knee and right hand together, right knee and left hand together). You will have to use your child as a model in order to get the proper spacing. To help teach left and right, draw a large "L" and "R" in the appropriate circles on the paper and put similarly marked masking tape on the back of your child's hands.

15b. As a variation of this exercise, have the child crawl backwards in a cross pattern. On request, the child should be able to name the hand he is using.

16. Have your child alternately stretch and relax various parts of his body: "Bend forward as far as you can." ". . . backward." "Make yourself as tall as you can. You can use your arms, too." "Now make yourself loose and floppy like a Raggedy Ann doll (or a towel)." "Now make believe you're a wooden soldier and you're stiff and hard." "See if you can blow yourself up a bit, like a balloon." "Now let the air out of the balloon a little bit at a time." "Make the balloon blow up again. Hold it. Now make believe I stuck a pin in the balloon. Show me what would happen if I did."

17. Place a "target" (a piece of colored paper 2″ or 3″ in diameter will do) on the wall about a foot from the floor. Instruct the child to move toward the target while keeping his eyes fixed on it. Make it a challenge: "Can you reach the mark on the wall by dragging yourself on your stomach?" or, ". . . without using your hands?" ". . . without using your hands or knees?" "Can you reach the mark while you're lying on your back?" "How many other ways can you reach the mark?"

18. The game of "Freeze" is a good one to use in teaching body awareness and control. Have your child move in time to music, skipping (not all pre-first-graders can skip) or dancing. Stop the music unexpectedly and at the same time say, "Freeze!" The child must stop, keeping his body in whatever position it was when you gave the command. Call attention to his position. Describe it and ask the child, "Where are your arms, feet, etc." Use a mirror.

19. The game of "Simon Says" develops the same skills as "Freeze" and can be used as an alternative.

20. Skipping rope is difficult for a child to do by himself. If there is another person to help you turn the rope for him, the same skills are taught, it's more fun and it's less frustrating. You can also attach one end of the rope to a fixed point and turn the other.

21. "Balance beam" activities are excellent. You can make a

balance beam quite easily. Get a 10′ or 12′ length of 2x4 from the lumber dealer. Tell him you want one that's "clear" (has no knots) and straight. It should be finished on all four sides so that it's smooth. Sand the 2x4 smoother and then put 2 or 3 coats of clear finish or enamel on it so that there's no danger of splinters. That's important because balance beam exercises are much more productive if they're done in stocking feet so your child is aware of the sensations coming from his feet. When the beam is ready, lay it flat on the floor and you're ready to begin the exercises. Later on, as the child becomes more proficient, the beam should be put on supports to raise it off the floor a few inches. (Three 18″ lengths of 4x6 can be notched to serve as braces.) Eventually the beam should be turned on edge—with supports, of course.

There are many balance beam exercises, but you should begin with the most straightforward ones: In all cases, affix a target (see Ex. 17) at eye level on which the child is to fix his eyes as he walks the beam. Have him move slowly. Maintaining balance is more important than speed.

A. "Start at this end of the beam and see if you can reach the other end." You will observe gradual improvement. Hold his hand to help balance, but remove the support as soon as possible.

B. "See if you can walk all the way to the other end backwards."

C. "Can you walk sideways?" Don't forget the target.

D. "Now try to get to the other end by crawling on your hands and knees."

E. "Can you think of any other ways to move from this end to the other?" Accept and encourage any variation.

F. When the child is quite proficient, have him carry something as he walks the beam. At first equal weights in each hand, then vary the weights to throw his center of balance off.

G. "Step onto the beam. Walk like an Indian, heel to toe, along the beam. Now try to walk the beam standing straight, looking at the target at the end of the beam. Keep your eyes on the target."

H. "This time while you're walking spread your arms out at your sides like a tightrope walker and move them slowly up and down as if you were flying. Look at the target. You can see your hands and arms moving up and down out of the corner of your eyes."

I. "Walk forward to the end of the beam, then backward

toe to heel fashion. Keep your eyes on the target. Don't peek over your shoulder. Try to remember where the end of the beam is. Watch the length of the beam in front of you as you walk backward so that you can guess when you'll come to the end."

J. "Walk backward Indian fashion. Wave your arms up and down slowly at your side and 'see' them out of the corners of your eyes."

K. Forward and backward walk. "Walk forward on the beam until I say REVERSE, then walk backwards until I tell you FORWARD again."

Ka. "Continue walking forward. Do this heel to toe Indian walk. Ready: Forward, reverse, forward. Watch your target."

For additional activities for the balance beam and the rocking board, refer to Perception Development Research Associates. Their address follows this section.

22. A "rocking board" is another easily constructed item of equipment. You'll need a piece of plywood ½" thick and about 18" square. Center a 4" length of 4x4 post on one side of the piece of plywood and attach it with wood screws which have the type of head that can be countersunk. Ask the man in the hardware store about this. On the other side of the plywood put non-skid tape of the type you can buy to put on the floor of a shower or the kind that is used on stair treads.

The idea of the rocking or balance board is to see how well and in how many different positions the child can remain on the board. Use your, and his, imagination and or refer to the Handbook mentioned above. As with the balance beam, help should be given only as long as absolutely necessary.

23. The game of "Hopscotch" is an excellent aid also, in training visual perception and balance. In addition, the basic skills of sequencing actions and counting are developed.

24. Hopping aids in developing balance and can also be used as an aid in teaching left and right. "Hop toward me on your left foot. Hop back to where you were on your right foot." If there's confusion, use the masking tape with "L" and "R" on hands and shoes. Give a variety of commands, such as alternating left and right, but don't try to confuse your child.

25. Simple commands, such as "Raise your left arm." "Bend your right knee." "Turn your head to the left." "Look to

the left" also teach directionality and aid in body awareness.

26. Combine training in motor control with training in sequencing. Say, "First take two steps forward and then take two steps back." As the child gets better doing this, go to a three step command. "Put the book on the chair, put the pencil on top of the book and hop to the door on your right foot," etc.

27. If you have access to a chalkboard and chalk, the following exercise will develop so-called "bilateral" skill. If no chalkboard is available, butcher paper and crayon will do. If neither of these is handy, go through the motions as though there were a chalkboard or paper. Have your child draw a large circle using full arm motion, first with one arm and then with the other and then with both arms together.

28. Play a game of catch with your child. Start with an 8" or 10" ball thrown from a distance of about 6 feet. Decrease the size of the ball and increase the distance gradually. The child should be successfull at least 7 out of 10 throws.

29. Leap frog is a good aid in developing body image.

30. Variations of the "Angels in the Snow" game are fine for teaching both body image and directionality.

   a. Have your child lie on his back with feet together and arms close to his sides.

   b. Next have him move both arms until his hands meet above his head. The arms should be kept stiff and remain touching the floor as he does this. Help him if he can't do it alone.

   c. Now have him keep his legs on the floor and move them as far apart as he can. Again, help may be needed.

   d. The next step is to have him do both arm and leg movements at the same time.

   e. When "a" through "d" have been mastered, and movements are smooth, try right and left identification. Say, "Move your left arm above your head. Remember to keep your arms stiff and on the floor. Now move just your left leg as far to the side as you can. Keep it stiff and on the floor." Do the same with both arms and legs. You may need to touch and actually move the arm or leg at first. Try to get the child to respond if you only point when you give the command. This may take some time. Be patient.

   f. When exercise "e" has been mastered, the next step is

to have right arm and leg moved together and left arm and leg move together. Then proceed to,

g. Cross pattern movements: right arm and left leg, and vice versa. Gradually increase the speed of movement.

h. Finally, have the child lie across a chair and perform the cross pattern movement, first on his back, and then on his stomach. The exercise must be brief. A couple of minutes is enough.

31. A barrel with the ends removed is a good addition to your equipment and should be used alone, or as part of the obstacle course suggested earlier. It can be tumbled or jumped over, or crawled through forward and backward.

32. Exercises involving somersaults and rolling are good for developing a sense of relationship to space. The eyes should be kept open while performing these. A well developed sense of spatial relationship helps eliminate problems of reversal so common to first graders, that is, mistaking "b" for "d" or "p" for "q".

We have suggested enough activities so that there should be no need to risk boredom by using the same one too frequently. That there are some thirty exercises is not an indication that they should be administered one-a-day, like vitamins. Repetition can be productive. Stay with one exercise until at least a reasonable degree of proficiency has been attained. The sense of satisfaction at having met a challenge successfully will encourage your child to stay with your program of exercises.

If your child can successfully perform all the exercises listed here, the odds are high that his sense of body image and his ability to control his body are well-developed.

The activities listed here are only a representative few of the many things you can do. Following are some sources of additional activities. Although some are geared to school use, they are also appropriate for parents.

1. Braley, William T., Konichi, Geraldine, and Leedy, Catherine. *Daily Sensorimotor Training Activities. A Handbook for Teachers and Parents of Pre-School Children.* Freeport, L.I., N.Y.: Education Activities, P.O. Box 392. 1968. Cost: $4.95.

   A book of activities designed to enhance perceptual awareness and develop motor ability in young children. Activities are listed by perceptual abilities which can be reinforced at home. A good resource for parents.

2. Capon, Jack J. *Perceptual Motor Development.* A series of five books for pre-school and elementary grades is now available from Fearon Publishers, 6 Davis Dr., Belmont, California 94002. 1975.

Cost: $3.00 each.

Book 1-Basic Movement Activities
Book 2-Ball, Rope, Hoop Activities
Book 3-Balance Activities
Book 4-Bean Bags, Rhythm Stick Activities
Book 5-Tire, Parachute Activities

The activites are organized for easy use. Tasks are arranged in logical sequence. The author has actually used the activities with children over a period of eight years.

3. Capon, Jack J. *Perceptual-Motor Lesson Plans.* Front Row Experience, Suite 213, 564 Central Avenue, Alameda, California 94501. 1975. Cost: $4.75.

Tested and proven perceptual-motor activities sequenced according to difficulty. Program developed in the Alameda Unified School District and refined over a period of eight years. Book also contains equipment sources and construction plans.

4. Cratty, Bryant J. *Developmental Sequences of Perceptual-Motor Tasks.* Educational Activities, P.O. Box 392, Freeport, L.I., N.Y. Cost: $2.95.

Movement activities are sequenced and listed under specific perceptual-motor characteristics.

5. Frostig, Marianne *Move-Grow-Learn.* Follett Educational Corporation, P.O. Box 5705, Chicago, Illinois 60680. 1969. Cost: $9.96.

Designed for school use, but can be used at home. Contains manual along with 181 exercise cards for teaching movement skills to pre-school, kindergarten, and primary grade children. The program is designed to enhance the total development of young children. Activities are very basic, easy to interpret and practical for implementation.

6. Hackett, Layne C. and Jenson, Robert G. *A Guide to Movement Exploration.* Peek Publications, Box 11065, Palo Alto, CA 94306. 1966.

A discussion of the goals of movement exploration. Describes procedures for using implements such as balls, hoops, ropes, tires, etc. Includes training plans for ages 5 to 12.

7. McCulloch, Lovell *A Handbook for Developing Perceptual-Motor and Sensory Skills Through Body Movement.* Austin Writers Group, P.O. Box 12642, Capitol Station, Austin Texas, 78711. 1973. Cost: $6.95.

8. O'Quinn, Garland *Gymnastics for Elementary School Children.* University Stores, Inc., P.O. Box 1441, Austin, Texas 78767. 1973. Cost: $4.95.

Gives step-by-step directions for using a variety of low cost motor activity equipment items. Explanations are brief and easy to follow. There are also excellent illustrations. Activities are carefully sequenced to insure positive results.

9. Stein, Joe *Head Over Heels.* Enrichment Materials Company, P.O. Box 812, Campbell, CA 1963

   A progression in tumbling and mat experiences for children grades K-8 is listed by developmental steps.

10. *Improving Motor-Perceptual Skills.* Division of Continuing Education, Oregon State System of Higher Education, Waldo Hall 100, Corvallis, Oregon 97331. 1970. Cost: $3.00.

    This is a step-by-step guide which provides directions for 34 activities to increase children's motor and perceptual skills. The activities are grouped into four categories: general coordination, balance, body image and eye-hand coordination.

SPECIAL NOTATION: The prices listed are approximate.

For those readers who have older children in need of developing body image and body control, an excellent source of information relative to activities is the following:

Perception Development Research Associates
Post Office Box 936
La Porte, Texas 77571

Mr. Frank Belgau, the head of this group, has worked extensively with and instructed at the University of Houston. Especially useful is their *Handbook of Training Activities*, which sells for about $5.00.

Refer also to the book by Joe Stein, listed above.

Bibliography

Chapter 1

Blackwood, Ralph O., *Operant Control of Behavior: Elimination of Misbehavior and Motivation of Children*, Ohio, Exordium Press, 1971.

Slobin, Dan I., *Psycholinguistics*, Illinois, Scott Foresman, 1971, p. 49.

Ibid., p. 50.

Chapter 5

McCall's Magazine, "Right Now" column, December, 1973.

Simon, Sidney B., et al., *Values Clarification, A Handbook of Practical Strategies for Teachers and Students*, New York, Hart Publishing Company Inc., 1972.

Chapter 6

Dreikurs, Rudolf, M.D. with Soltz, Vicki, R.N., *Children: The Challenge*, New York, Hawthorne Books, Inc., 1964.

Chapter 7

Gunther, Bernard, *Sense Relaxation Below Your Mind*, New York, Pocket Books, 1973, preface.

Chapter 8

Harris, Thomas A., M.D., *I'm OK, You're OK: A Practical Guide to Transactional Analysis*, New York, Harper and Row, 1967.

Maslow, Abraham, *Toward a Psychology of Being*, Princeton, New Jersey, Van Nostrand, 1962.

Mussen, Paul H., *The Psychological Development of the Child*, New York, Prentice-Hall, 1963, p. 72.

Rogers, Carl R., *On Becoming a Person*, Boston, Houghton Mifflin, 1961.

Chapter 9

Combs, Arthur W. and Snygg, Donald, *Individual Behavior*, New York, Harper and Brothers, 1959, p. 229.

Tubesing, Donald A. and Nancy L., *Tune In*, Milwaukee, Wisconsin, Listening Group, 1973, p. 29.

Chapter 10

Combs, Arthur W. and Snygg, Donald, *Individual Behavior*, New York, Harper and Brothers, 1959, pp. 244-245.

Maslow, Abraham H., *Motivation and Personality*, New York, Harper, 1954, pp. 388-389.

Porter, Elias H., *An Introduction to Therapeutic Counseling*, Boston, Houghton Mifflin, 1950.

Tubesing, Donald A. and Nancy L., *Tune In*, Milwaukee, Wisconsin, Listening Group, 1973, p. 44.

Chapter 11

Webster's Collegiate Dictionary, Fifth Edition, Springfield, Massachusetts, G. & C. Merriam Co. 1947.

Chapter 12

Dreikurs, Rudolph, M.D. with Soltz, Vicki, R.N., *Children: The Challenge*, New York, Hawthorne Books, 1964, p. 282.

About the Author

Thomas G. Banville has had broad experience in both educational psychology and psychological counseling. As a psychoeducational specialist he has served as a consultant to a number of school systems on problems related to language development and learning. He has worked for the California and Nevada Departments of Mental Hygiene, and he has been responsible for the evaluation of federal programs in education. His counseling experience includes work with students from kindergarten through twelfth grade, and private practice in marriage and family counseling.

Dr. Banville is a widely published writer, whose articles have appeared in such magazines as *Instructor, American Education, Education Digest, P.T.A., Modern Romances, Nevada Highways* and *Essence*. He is also a regular contributor to *Early Years*.

Dr. Banville's doctoral work was done in the area of perception and he is the developer of the Perceptual Development Quick Test.